Reach

Destiny Awaits

Debra A. Allen

Reach

Cover Design: Debi Bolocofsky

Printed in the United States of America

Faith-to-Faith

ISBN 978-0-9764914-1-5

Dedication

I would like to dedicate this book to my family, my spiritual sons and daughters, and those who have encouraged and supported me in the ministry. May the blessings and favor of God always be with you.

ACKNOWLEDGMENTS

Special thanks to my daughters Stephanie, Chandria, and my niece, Diondra, for their support and work in the ministry. Thank you for providing the quiet moments needed to write.

For my spiritual sons and daughters that provide oversight to various ministries in the US and abroad, thank you for being a ray of sunlight. I am so proud of you and the work that you do for the kingdom. Your love, prayers, and continual support mean so much to me.

Thank you New Hope World Outreach, the Ministerial Council, and ESP Team I appreciate your faithfulness, dedication, prayers, support, and work that you do. You are a blessing to the kingdom and me.

I am truly thankful for Apostles Ruby and Robert Green for their wisdom, faith, and prayers that undergird and support me.

To my special Arkansas prayer partner, Nina Townsend and family, thank you so much for your love, prayers, my special couch, and place of peace. Special thanks to the Brassfields, Phil, Terry, and Ken (deceased), who were also there for me through the era of this book. I am forever grateful to all of you. You are always in my heart and prayers.

TABLE OF CONTENTS

INTRODUCTION

Often I would sit and look at the waters, the deep calling unto deep. The stillness of the moment or the roaring waves beating against the sand consoles me. As each wave of the sea rippled and water washed upon the beach, a little more of the pain flowed out with the waves. The healing process began that day.

It seems there are so many questions that must be answered for true inner healing to occur. A series of questions rush through my mind. Where is my joy? James 1:2 tells me to "Count it all joy." How can I have joy when there is so much pressing on me and weighing me down? In such anguish, I cry out, "Can't you see I am in such pain? How can I live?" Jesus gave me the answer, and it is very simple: "Live each day in Christ."

In Him, in Christ, there is life. The road to recovery requires one to live one day at a time and one step at a time. There are no magical formulas for restoration. However, the Bible states in Acts 17:28, *"For in him we live, and move, and have our being."* The key is you must be in Him. In Him is a wonderful place of peace and rest. Through it all, the blood of the Lamb redeems and comforts us.

Only Jesus could pay the price to redeem us back from the depths of hell. He gave His life so that we could live. Jesus stated in John 10:10-11, *"I am come that they might have life, and that they might have it more abundantly. I am the good shepherd: the good shepherd giveth his life for the sheep."* Jesus, the good shepherd, gave His life so that you and I could have an abundant life.

As you read the pages of this book, you will discover that you can have that abundant life only the Redeemer, the

Holy One of Israel can give. Also, you will receive strength and encouragement as you discover the truth of God's Word and the relationship He so desires to have with you. One important thing that I discovered over the years is that the greatest gift I have ever received came from Jesus. You may think I am talking about salvation. However, salvation is just the beginning. Living daily in Him represents completion. The greatest benefit that you will receive from this book is the ability to live again. Do not give up! Jesus of Nazareth is passing by, and all you have to do is simply--**REACH**.

CHAPTER ONE
A CRY FOR HELP

I must tell Jesus all of my trials; I cannot bear these burdens alone; In my distress He kindly will help me; He ever loves and cares for His own (Hoffman, E. A. 1893).

Over the years, I have discovered such great comfort can come from a song. When I need an answer or encouragement or simply a change of direction, a song comes up in my spirit, and I begin to hum the tune. As I stop and listen to what I am humming, I realize the words to the song have a message. I find comfort in what my spirit is saying to me by the Holy Spirit because my answer is in the song.

I must tell Jesus was my heart's cry for so long. Distress was what I was feeling along with pain, anxiety, sorrow, mental anguish, and trapped. The choices we make in life can make us go spiraling down a path that does not lead to "happily ever after." So often, we are unable to get a breakthrough in a situation because we have not faced the problem nor accepted the truth about the problem. Most people, when they are "going through" as we call it, are usually in denial. They put on a happy face to camouflage the pain or hide the shame. That was my plight.

I grew up in the church. I had a solid foundation in the Word of God and a good relationship with Him. I knew I had a calling on my life and I was active in the ministry. In 1987, I said, "I do" for the second time. The invitation read I am marrying my best friend. Surely, this was the one. When you are dating, the individuals involved put their best foot forward. You get to know the person after you say I do. Little by little, I learned the character and true nature of the best friend.

Have you ever felt that life is like a roller coaster? There are highs and lows, twists and turns, ups and downs, and don't forget those incredible loops where you turn upside down.

For eight years, I was on a roller coaster in my marriage, and I felt the ride would never end. So, I sought counsel from my pastor and others in Christ. Stay, don't go, go, don't stay was the type of advice I received. The answer would change depending upon who talked to me. I never will forget one Saturday morning I was sitting in my pastor's living room seeking answers. He simply said, "Do you think you married the wrong person?" My pastor was not recommending divorce; he saw me struggling with my faith to stay or go. He needed me to examine my decision up to that point. It was evident to my pastor that we were unequally yoked. Only one person came to counseling. Apparently, no support system was in place that he could observe.

By this time, I felt trapped in a valley of decision and unable to make a clean break. I kept trying to exercise my faith in the marriage and just believe God for a miracle. You may say you are a minister and a person of faith. How did this happen to you? Could you not believe God for your marriage? Yes, and I did for eight years. I prayed diligently for the marriage and my husband. I walked by faith, and I confessed faith words. I felt there was nothing that my faith in God and prayer could not do. However, you cannot change a person's will. He or she will have to be willing to change, and God will work with them.

Too many times, we cover up the true hurt or hide behind our work, our careers, our lives, or our families only to avoid the inevitable, the pain. We simply survive day to day, but we do not truly live. God does not want us just to survive. He wants us to live the abundant life that came from Jesus. He does not want us to live below the promises but inherit them. Like others around me, I was in a survival mode for many of those eight years.

Survival mode does not produce the results that God intended for us. He no longer wants us to camouflage our hurts and pains. He wants to expose the hurt and pain so that He may "set us free." The only way to be free from pain is to walk in truth. John 8:32 states, *"And ye shall know the truth, and the truth shall make you free."* Acknowledging the truth is the beginning of recovery and the road to victory. Faith is the door into the realm of blessings and freedom. All you have to do is tell Jesus everything.

The Turning Point

Some people stay in a bad marriage for all the wrong reasons. I wanted to stay, but to live I had to go. Time was of the essence. Oppression was weighing me down. Like David did in Psalms 34:4, *"I sought the LORD, and he heard me, and delivered me from all my fears."* I will never forget the turning point in my life. On this particular day, I was sitting in my living room in such a state of oppression. Why was I oppressed? Because I had stayed too long in a situation that was not going to change, I felt disappointed and angry. I had waited for God to perform a miracle on this man. However, my hopes for a "they lived happily ever after life" dashed to the ground. All I could hear in the background was the controlling, nagging, and tormenting demonic spirit operating in my husband

3

with a vengeance. The demonic force in him was on an assignment to kill me through oppression and depression. The intent was to get me down physically and emotionally. Perhaps the goal was to have me give up and die on the inside. I remember how he was pacing, talking, and raging. I guess the Holy Ghost had enough because deep within me, out of my belly, there surged a response that shattered the spirit realm. I cried with a loud voice, "I want to live!" The Holy Ghost and the angelic force were waiting to hear my cry. Something snapped in the spirit realm, and I was no longer bound. You see the answer did not have anything to do with marriage. It was about life.

The words of this song, *I Must Tell Jesus*, so clearly described how I felt during the storm and on the road to recovery. We all feel, at different times in our lives, distressed, perplexed, angry, frustrated, and rejected. Under pressure from external forces and internal turmoil, pain and fear grip our hearts. Agonizing from the pain of rejection and overcome by grief, we feel despondent. We cry, why me, or why is this happening to me? Desperate for an answer, a simple solution to troubled times we continue to cry out. In the midst of the storm, we cry, is anyone there?

When God broke that spirit of control, I was no longer under the influence of the enemy. I could see clearly and think clearly. More importantly, I was no longer in denial nor fooled by all the signs of infidelity that were staring me in the face. It was as if life rushed back into me. I can truly say that God walked me through this difficult time in my life through His Word and His indwelling presence. Joshua 1:5 and Psalms 27 were scriptures used to comfort me for the journey that was ahead. Joshua 1:5 states, *"There shall not any man be able to stand before thee all the days of thy life: as I was with Moses, so I will be with thee: I will not fail thee, nor forsake thee."* Since God

4

does not lie and He honors His word, I knew I would never be alone.

The key to receiving this promise of Joshua 1:5 was for me to get to a place called "there." For the children of Israel, they had to go over Jordan to get to the land God promised them. They could not stay where they were mourning the death of Moses forever nor could they lament about the past and all they enjoyed previously. Looking back over the past produces regret.

Where was my "there?" My there was not a physical place. It was a place of rekindled faith and trust in the power of God to help me. I had to get back to that secret place in God that Psalms 91:1-4 describes:

"He that dwelleth in the secret place of the most High shall abide under the shadow of the Almighty. I will say of the Lord, He is my refuge and my fortress: my God; in him will I trust. Surely he shall deliver thee from the snare of the fowler, and from the noisome pestilence. He shall cover thee with his feathers, and under his wings shalt thou trust: his truth shall be thy shield and buckler."

To rekindle my faith, I began to have that love for the Word of God again. I saturated myself with faith messages to restore my faith. I remember sitting in front of the TV with a recorder to capture every faith-filled message that Kenneth Copeland shared. I would play them over and over to encourage myself.

Faith to Leave

I knew a divorce was inevitable in this relationship, however, how or when was not clear. It was my youngest daughter, Chandria's, senior year and she was the valedictorian. I could not be selfish and take that from her trying to escape the marriage. Praying and seeking God were the answers. One evening, the pastor, his wife, and I were at the church praying for the upcoming services. I heard God distinctly say that He was sending me to Florida by the water, which I loved. All I had was a word from God. It was enough to sustain me because He knew the particulars of when, where, and how.

The life-changing events that took place over time were amazing. First, you cannot just pack up and leave without a plan; timing is everything. I knew no one in Florida nor did I know where to move. Nevertheless, God knows everything and absolutely nothing happens by chance. One of the members of my staff was browsing through the Chronicle of Higher Education and found a position open for an Associate Vice President of Technical Education at Broward Community College (BCC) in Fort Lauderdale, Florida. She said to me, "this job description sounds like you." One of the criteria was to work with the Tech Prep program. I wrote the grant and provided oversight for Tech Prep in our county. In 1995, there were 1,029 Tech Prep consortia in the US. Our college consortium, Mississippi County Tech Prep Consortium, had just won national recognition from the US Department of Education's Excellence in Tech Prep Award.

Working with grants was another requirement, and I had written grants for our college for the past 18 years. So, my staff member was right; the position was tailor-made for me. I applied for the position. During the interview, I found that two years earlier BCC advertised the position and withdrew it. The college could not find an acceptable candidate for the position. I believe God reserved that position for me so He could deliver me from bondage. By August, my youngest daughter attended Texas A&M University on a valedictorian scholarship, my oldest

6

daughter entered the veterinarian program at the University of Florida, and I headed to Ft. Lauderdale, Florida to begin the next phase of my career at BCC. God put all those wonderful pieces of the puzzle together and divinely orchestrated our lives.

While God was working all these details out, behind the scene, I relied heavily on the Word of God for answers. I recalled, throughout history, God always delivered His people. During the time of famine, the children of Israel moved to Egypt and enjoyed life because their brother, Joseph, was governor. God had granted Joseph great favor, and he was in a position to help his people.

Through the wisdom of God, Joseph was able to provide for the country and his family. Before Joseph died, he told the children of Israel *"God will surely visit you, and bring you out of this land unto the land which he sware to Abraham, to Isaac, and to Jacob" (Gen. 50:24).* Joseph understood, by the Spirit, that God would deliver Israel from the hands of the Egyptians.

Over the course of time, Joseph died, and there arose a new Pharaoh over Egypt who did not know Joseph. The new Pharaoh enslaved the children of Israel. However, they cried out to God for help. They were afflicted, oppressed, discouraged, and bound. It is oppressive to be subject unto or controlled by someone or something. No one wants to be a slave, whether in the natural or in the spirit. When the burden became unbearable, they sought help from God. The entire book of Exodus records how God brought them out of bondage with a mighty outstretched arm.

What kept them so long in Egypt? Could it be they were content to stay in the situation because change requires action? Can you imagine their predicament? Under the

7

leadership of Joseph, they enjoyed the best. They had favor, prestige, honor, and freedom. I wonder why they did not leave Egypt when Joseph died. There was nothing to keep them there. Their relative was dead, and they were free men. At any point in time, before the new Pharaoh, they could have left; yet they stayed. Could it be that they were comfortable with their arrangement under Joseph's leadership? Unfortunately, they stayed so long in Egypt they forgot it was not the land of promise. Egypt was not their destination; it was simply a place of refuge in a time of famine. However, when they became grieved, provoked, and angered by their plight, they sought God.

Often our lives or situations are pretty much like the plight of the children of Israel. We stay too long on a job or in a bad relationship because of familiarity and complacency. Fear of the unknown binds us to unhealthy relationships or situations. We would not normally stay in those situations. I often wonder about how different the chain of events would have been if Israel left Egypt the moment Joseph died. Do you wonder about your life? How different would it have been had you taken a specific turn or gone down a certain path?

Like many of us, the children of Israel stayed too long in Egypt, and now a cruel taskmaster enslaved them. Bitter and saddened over such bondage, they cried out to God. *"And God heard their groaning, and God remembered his covenant with Abraham, with Isaac, and with Jacob. And God looked upon the children of Israel, and God had respect unto them" (Ex. 2:24-25).* Their sorrows moved God's heart, and He remembered the covenant He made with Abraham. Now it was time to fulfill the promise. Notice how the children of Israel did not cry out to God until it became unbearable for them to stay in Egypt. God did not intervene until asked.

When I was seeking God about what I should do about my marriage, I was waiting for a specific answer. I was waiting to hear everything would be fine and that my husband would change. At first, I was so embarrassed and ashamed when I would faithfully go to church, minister the Word, and he did not attend. The only comfort I received was the Holy Ghost said, "You are only responsible for yourself, not the action of others." This word of encouragement gave me the strength to hold my head up and continue working in the ministry. Sometimes I thought about what others were saying, but you cannot let that stop you from doing what is right.

When God is for you, He is more than the world against you. Nothing can alter God's love nor His willingness to deliver His children. Just as Joseph stated, God had a plan for delivering the children of Israel from Egypt. He was preparing His servant, Moses, to lead them.

God revealed His plan of action to Moses. His assignment was to speak to Pharaoh on behalf of the children of Israel and bring them out of Egypt. Under great pressure, Pharaoh released the Israelites and Moses brought the people out. Deuteronomy 26:7-9 states:

7 And when we cried unto the LORD God of our fathers, the LORD heard our voice, and looked on our affliction, and our labour, and our oppression: 8 And the LORD brought us forth out of Egypt with a mighty hand, and with an outstretched arm, and with great terribleness, and with signs, and with wonders: 9 And he hath brought us into this place, and hath given us this land, even a land that floweth with milk and honey.

God knows what it takes to deliver us. He removes all obstacles and barriers to get results. He has people in place praying for you. Mentally, leaving Blytheville,

9

Arkansas and that marriage was not easy. God used my sister, Apostle Ruby Green, and my oldest daughter, Stephanie, who was 22 as my Moses. They stood in the gap and made up the hedge for me in great prayer and intercession to be free by the Spirit. Two days before I was to leave Blytheville and start my new life in Florida, my sister was engaged in such spiritual warfare for me. She interceded before the throne of Grace to break that spirit of control from me until whelps appeared upon her body. The intercession had such a great impact on my daughter. She realized the seriousness of the matter when she witnessed the intensity of that prayer. God used Stephanie to continue to pray for me, in the Spirit, as she drove 70 miles from Memphis to Blytheville.

When my daughter described the spiritual warfare that took place, I knew I was in serious trouble. Have you ever had the feeling that you were part of something going on, but you were an observer, and it was not happening to you? I felt like this as she described the chain of events. I was standing on the outside looking at my life and my predicament while watching things unravel before me.

When you are in bondage, you may not know how badly you are in bondage or how to get out of Egypt, which is not as simple as one thinks. Some stay in situations because of financial security, familiarity, complacency, children, family, fear, control, and just bound. I stayed because I was still trying to hold onto a hopeless situation and I needed to be free. I left because God heard my cry and He delivered me.

The Healing

There is only one doctor, one great physician who can heal any sickness, disease, or emotional hurt. Jesus can heal all brokenness; He alone has the answer and the cure. A very familiar adage says, "Time heals all wounds." Rose Kennedy, mother of John and Robert Kennedy, refuted that statement. She stated, *"It has been said, 'time heals all wounds.' I do not agree. The wounds remain. In time, the mind, protecting its sanity, covers them with scar tissue and the pain lessens. But it is never gone"* *(Kennedy, n.d.).* I believe it takes more than time for healing to occur after divorce, hurt, and pain. It takes the power and love of God.

After I moved to Florida, I recall many days and nights I would sit alone on my balcony overlooking the water. Staring into the midst, I expected the ripple of the water to wash away my pain. I felt the emotional strain of a diminishing relationship. Grief, guilt, and shame took turns trying to overcome me. I was so angry for finding myself in this position of another divorce. I agonized over what went wrong and wondered could I have done anything differently. One night, God had me to sit down and write and write and write out all my frustration and anger. He had me to start the exercise by writing at the top of the page I am so angry "because" and list everything. Many tear-stained pages later, I was able to let it go.

The words to my song helped me, and the power of a loving Savior healed me. *"I must tell Jesus all of my trials; I cannot bear these burdens alone; In my distress He kindly will help me; He ever loves and cares for His own"* *(Scriven).* If you listen, I mean really listen, you will hear *"He ever loves and cares for His own."* Jesus' love declares I am with you always. I understand. I forgive. I will not forsake you. I will not reject you. You are not alone. Do you have a song, saying, or favorite scripture that comforts you? The following scripture reminds me that things happen in life, but we are victorious in Christ.

When thou passest through the waters, I will be with thee; and through the rivers, they shall not overflow thee: when thou walkest through the fire, thou shalt not be burned; neither shall the flame kindle upon thee. For I am the LORD thy God, the Holy One of Israel, thy Saviour: I gave Egypt for thy ransom, Ethiopia and Seba for thee. Since thou wast precious in my sight, thou hast been honourable, and I have loved thee: therefore will I give men for thee, and people for thy life. Fear not: for I am with thee: (Is. 43:2-5).

You see the scripture states when you pass through the waters. It is not if you pass through the waters of difficult times but a definite when you do. We all go through things in life that only the power of God can walk us through; it is called trials and tribulations. The comfort and assurance are that God will be with us according to Isaiah. Furthemore, in John 16:33, Jesus stated, *"These things I have spoken unto you, that in me ye might have peace. In the world ye shall have tribulation: but be of good cheer; I have overcome the world."* Jesus' victory on the cross produces overcoming power in us. Do not ever underestimate the power of God's love nor the saving grace of Jesus Christ. Fear not, God can reach you where you are.

CHAPTER TWO
IT'S A DIVORCE--NOT TREASON

The most important thing you should know is this: your circumstance, your situation, nor your sin shock God. God is omnipotent and omniscient. He is all-powerful, and He knows all things. Do not think for a moment that your situation is unique. Solomon tells us in Ecclesiastes 1:9, *"The thing that hath been, it is that which shall be; and that which is done is that which shall be done: and there is no new thing under the sun."*

There is no new thing under the sun. Whatever you are experiencing, someone else before you went through the situation. From Genesis to Revelation, if you will take the time to read the Word, you will understand how to come out of the situation or how to overcome the barriers. Remember, the *"Truth shall make you free" (Jn. 8:32).* The truth of the Word will liberate you and help you LIVE.

When the Holy Ghost gave me the topics to discuss in this book, He made a profound statement. He said to me, "Divorce is not an act of treason; Divorce is a breach of a promise." Breach means something has occurred that caused a gap or a break. A breach in the relationship indicates that the original promise is no longer intact. Treason, on the other hand, is a violation of allegiance to one's sovereign or one's state (dictionary.com, 2017). Those of us that have divorced did not violate our allegiance to God. We did not offend God or have a breach in our relationship with Him. Many people have found themselves in such great bondage and guilt about divorce. They cannot seem to rise above the stigma associated with a divorce. A dark cloud looms over them echoing - failure, failure, failure. At first, that was me. I was one of those statistics included in the failed marriage category. What happened?

Did you have any signs that this may not be the right one? Yes! The weekend of the wedding, a friend flew in to surprise me. When I saw her, I cried hysterically. It was not because of joy. I think it was the feeling in my gut. It was telling me I was making a mistake. Should I have called off the wedding? Why didn't I call off the wedding and save myself years of grief?

After the first divorce, I said I was not getting married again. When I introduced the new love to my mother, she later said I thought you were not getting married again. What did she see that I did not see? There is a saying that love is blind. Is it? All I know is that immediately after saying I do, the blinders came off and I knew. Pride did not let me follow the signs beforehand and call that wedding off.

Dealing with Grief

At the root of grief is anger. Grief comes from the Hebrew word, ka'ac, which means vexation: --anger, indignation, provocation, sorrow, and wrath (Strong's Talking Greek & Hebrew Dictionary, 2017). When wronged, people respond in several ways. First, there is anger, then suppression of true feelings, followed by denial. All of these emotions lead to grief.

Grief is a monster and a strong force. It must be acknowledged and dealt with immediately. Many people associate grief with dying. Dying is the obvious form of grief. Examples of grief may be a mother mourning for a

14

child, a husband for his wife, a student for a classmate, or a little child for a beloved pet. I have read that the grieving process is healthy. Prolonged states of grief, however, are deadly. Depression sets in and a person may require medical attention. Grief is not healthy. Sometimes the grieving party longs to die as well.

What occurs during the grieving process? A series of emotions arise through one's grief. The person may experience guilt. When a person dies, it is so final. There are no more opportunities to reconcile a bad relationship. When there are harsh words spoken before death, one does not have an opportunity to say, I'm sorry, please forgive me. Instead of denial, a person must face the fact that the loved one is gone. A divorce is like death; it too is final.

I never will forget when my mother died. I was away on a business trip. The night before, I had an urge to pray. I prayed, but I did not get a clear understanding of what I was praying about or for whom I was praying. That night, I went with colleagues to dinner and did not give it another thought. The next day I learned my mother had passed away in her sleep. It was such a shock. I distinctly remember telling a friend that Jesus did not tell me my mother was going to die. I remember praying the night before; was that prayer for my mother or me?

During the funeral preparation, I remember being steady as a rock. It may have been weeks even months until reality hit. I was curling my hair and talking to Jesus. Like a bolt of lightning, the reality of my mother's death hit me. I had to talk it out. I told Jesus everything I needed to have said to my mother. In the back of my mind, I still pondered the night she died. Should I have prayed more? After emptying out the full range of emotions I was feeling, Jesus said let it go. In an instant, the grief broke.

Isn't it amazing what the subconscious will do? If anyone had told me I was grieving, I would have laughed. I was working and going through all the motions of living. I was very active, but I was also grieving. This same process of confessing all, discussing all, and letting go of all emotions associated with grief is required for anyone to heal. When someone offends, betrays, violates, wounds, or abuses, you experience anger. Why did they do that to me, you may ask? You try to guess their actions and figure out their motives. If you do not immediately relinquish the emotions, grief will overtake you. Grief then becomes a gamut of emotions all linked to the original anger.

When a person loses a loved one, he or she may get mad at God. Often people ask God, why did you take my loved one away? When a person is involved in any tragedy, they question the source of the tragedy. Jesus explains it this way *"The thief cometh not, but for to steal, and to kill, and to destroy: I am come that they might have life, and that they might have it more abundantly" (John 10:10)*. The thief is the devil, and his main mission is to kill and ultimately destroy. He will use grief to rob you of your joy and strength.

Grief may take many forms. When bombarded by a series of problems and disappointments, you grieve. A sudden or slow loss of finances causes grief. Breaking up from a relationship can cause grief. If you thrive on others and their approval and you do not get it, you experience grief. As pastors and ministers, we often offer advice to those we counsel. When they do not heed the sound advice and get in trouble or a tragedy occurs, we grieve.

The only way to overcome grief is to recognize that you are not responsible. You cannot be responsible for decisions others make or the road they take. So let go of

16

the guilt and live. Nehemiah 8:10 states, *"neither be ye sorry; for the joy of the LORD is your strength."* You must have strength to continue with life.

To regain the needed strength to live, we must forgive. As Christians, we often go through periods of offering lip service to forgiveness. We know the Word states we must forgive; so we say I forgive. However, forgiveness is not something you can assent to mentally. Forgiveness requires emptying out of the emotional baggage associated with unforgiveness. Also, forgiveness requires you to state by faith you forgive and forget.

Some people tell me I will forgive, but I will never forget what they did to me. I often ask do you need God to forgive you? The reply is always yes; I respond, you must forgive and forget. *"And when ye stand praying, forgive, if ye have ought against any: that your Father also which is in heaven may forgive you your trespasses. But if ye do not forgive, neither will your Father which is in heaven forgive your trespasses"* *(Mark 11:25-26)*. The situation or the circumstance does not matter; we must forgive to be forgiven. You may be convinced to forgive, but may ask, why do I need to forget? *"For I will be merciful to their unrighteousness, and their sins and their iniquities will I remember no more"* *(Heb. 8:12)*. When you ask God to forgive you, He does not remember you sin anymore. God forgives and forgets. If you do not forgive and forget, you suffer the consequences of your action.

Unforgiveness is not healthy. Many people become bitter, depressed, oppressed, and physically ill because they would not forgive. Can you afford to live with unforgiveness? Is it worth forfeiting your life? God will not forgive you if you do not forgive the one that offended you.

Jesus knew and practiced the spiritual principle of forgiveness. Upon Calvary's cross, He could have cursed the nation and condemned us all for our transgressions. However, Jesus practiced what he taught; He showed us how to forgive. When He died on the cross, He cried, *"Father, forgive them; for they know not what they do" (Lk. 23:34).* Jesus' cry was not lip service. From His spirit and heart, He showed grace and mercy upon the very ones who caused Him all the pain and grief. The people who crucified Him received forgiveness, simply because Jesus asked God to forgive them. His cry to God to forgive was a powerful example and testimony. Just follow Jesus' example-forgive.

Repent now from any unforgiveness you may have stored within your heart. Tell Jesus you forgive the person who wronged you. For help, pray Father, I understand that I must forgive if I want to receive forgiveness for all the things I have done. I must follow you, Lord Jesus. I alone am responsible for my actions. I choose to forgive and not take any more thought about the offense. I forgive myself also. Now Lord, help me to forget. Once you sincerely pray that simple prayer of repentance and forgiveness, you release the unforgiveness.

Freedom from unforgiveness is just one hurdle to cross. Consider the thoughts of failure that come to mind to dismay or discourage. In Deuteronomy 31:8, God stated, *"And the LORD, he it is that doth go before thee; he will be with thee, he will not fail thee, neither forsake thee: fear not, neither be dismayed."* Two things are necessary to counteract the thoughts of failure, fear not and do not be dismayed. Jesus wants you free.

Often, we let our thoughts or others' opinion condemn and keep us in bondage. Some people treat those who have divorced like criminals. Treason is a criminal offense. It
18

is an attempt to overthrow the government to which the offender owes allegiance. It represents betrayal. Contrary to other's belief, divorce is not some criminal offense against God. Individuals who are divorced have not betrayed God and the holy state of matrimony to which they owed allegiance.

The opinion of others cannot define nor condemn. God explicitly explains His intent for marriage. Deuteronomy 24:1-4 states:

24:1 When a man hath taken a wife, and married her, and it come to pass that she find no favour in his eyes, because he hath found some uncleanness in her: then let him write her a bill of divorcement, and give it in her hand, and send her out of his house.
2 And when she is departed out of his house, she may go and be another man's wife.
3 And if the latter husband hate her, and write her a bill of divorcement, and giveth it in her hand, and sendeth her out of his house; or if the latter husband die, which took her to be his wife;
4 Her former husband, which sent her away, may not take her again to be his wife, after that she is defiled; for that is abomination before the LORD: and thou shalt not cause the land to sin, which the LORD thy God giveth thee for an inheritance.

According to Deuteronomy 24:1-4, it was legal to get a divorce. In verse one, the woman found no favor in her husband's eyes because he had found some uncleanness in her. He no longer desired the woman as his wife. The bill of divorcement was the legal means to end the marriage. Before using a bill of divorcement, the husband would put the wife out of the home. He could wake up one morning and say I do not want you so get out and that would end the marriage. The woman may have loved the man and wanted to stay, but she had no choice. She was put away.

The bill of divorcement was intended to give some dignity to the woman and to provide proof that the man divorced her. It offered the woman a form of protection and legal clearance that she no longer belonged to the man. Verse two explains that the woman may go and be another man's wife. This verse answers the question, from the scripture, on whether one can remarry.

There may be a precedent set in this divorce and remarry cycle. Verse three explains that if the second husband hates her, he may put her away. However, the law states in verse four, that the first husband will cause the land to sin if he remarries his first wife after she has been the wife of another man. As you can see from the scriptures, the law regarding divorce was allowed because of the hardness of the people's heart. The motivation and reason for divorce were acts of convenience.

Let's look at the union of marriage spiritually with illustrations from the Word. The book of Hosea represents the condition of Israel in her pursuit of idols (lovers). Israel was constantly in a state of unfaithfulness. They followed the rules and customs of the people of the land and worshipped their gods. Their sons and daughters were allowed to marry strangers. To illustrate how these actions displeased God, He had the prophet Hosea, a holy man, marry a harlot, an unholy Gomer. Hosea 1:2-3 states:

2 The beginning of the word of the LORD by Hosea. And the LORD said to Hosea, Go, take unto thee a wife of whoredoms and children of whoredoms: for the land hath committed great whoredom, departing from the LORD.
3 So he went and took Gomer the daughter of Diblaim; which conceived, and bare him a son.

God used Gomer to represent the spiritual adultery that was rampant in Israel. They would go through seasons of following God. At other times, they sought other lovers and did everything except remain faithful to their first love and husband, Jehovah. The adultery God hates is the spiritual adultery (unfaithfulness) of His people. He often describes the unfaithfulness as playing the harlot. Hosea was instructed to forgive and redeem Gomer. In the preface to Hosea, it explains that Gomer was in slavery and had to be redeemed. Hosea 3:1-3 states:

3:1 Then said the LORD unto me, Go yet, love a woman beloved of her friend, yet an adulteress, according to the love of the LORD toward the children of Israel, who look to other gods, and love flagons of wine.
2 So I bought her to me for fifteen pieces of silver, and for an homer of barley, and an half homer of barley:
3 And I said unto her, Thou shalt abide for me many days; thou shalt not play the harlot, and thou shalt not be for another man: so will I also be for thee.

The constant idolatry, worshiping images, and taking the gods of other countries was vanity. The gods of the land would not be able to help Israel. The adoration Israel once had for Almighty God was now placed on carved images. Hosea 4:12-13 states the condition of Israel:

12 My people ask counsel at their stocks, and their staff declareth unto them: for the spirit of whoredoms hath caused them to err, and they have gone a whoring from under their God.
13 They sacrifice upon the tops of the mountains, and burn incense upon the hills, under oaks and poplars and elms, because the shadow thereof is good: therefore your daughters shall commit whoredom, and your spouses shall commit adultery.

The people violated the laws established by God and sacrificed to idols. Israel received commandments regarding the worship of God, which they violated. *"Thou shalt have no other gods before me. Thou shalt not make unto thee any graven image, or any likeness of any thing that is in heaven above, or that is in the earth beneath, or that is in the water under the earth:" (Ex. 20:3-4).*

This attitude of unfaithfulness prevailed throughout Israel. The consequences of Israel's adultery were a backslidden condition. They joined themselves to idols in an unholy relationship. Verse 17 states, *"Ephraim is joined to idols: let him alone."* Ephraim's unfaithfulness was serious; it indicated a yoke, a bond, and marriage to idols.

Spiritually speaking, matrimony is bondage when the yoke is unequal. It brings with it all the heartaches and grief that Hosea experienced in his marriage to Gomer. She was never satisfied with love. Always searching for something better, Gomer's lust could not be satisfied by one person. She sought many lovers.

Malachi 2:11 further explains the lusts and the spiritual condition of the children of Israel: *"Judah hath dealt treacherously, and an abomination is committed in Israel and in Jerusalem; for Judah hath profaned the holiness of the LORD which he loved, and hath married the daughter of a strange god."*

The yoke of a believer to an unbeliever is symbolic of verse 11 where Judah married the daughter of a strange god. Marriage is a covenant and a bond between two people. When a person joins with someone of another land, the spouse will entice him or her to serve his or her god. Israel was forbidden to enter into such unions. Exodus 34:15-16 states:

15 Lest thou make a covenant with the inhabitants of the land, and they go a whoring after their gods, and do sacrifice unto their gods, and one call thee, and thou eat of his sacrifice;
16 And thou take of their daughters unto thy sons, and their daughters go a whoring after their gods, and make thy sons go a whoring after their gods.

Israel would not listen. To please the spouse, the children of Israel broke the law and commandment of God. When they came into the land, they would put away the wife of their youth and take a stranger as a wife and his or her god. That is why Malachi strongly proclaimed God's great displeasure with putting away in Malachi 2:15-16:

15 And did not he make one? Yet had he the residue of the spirit. And wherefore one? That he might seek a godly seed. Therefore take heed to your spirit, and let none deal treacherously against the wife of his youth.
16 For the LORD, the God of Israel, saith that he hateth putting away: for one covereth violence with his garment, saith the LORD of hosts: therefore take heed to your spirit, that ye deal not treacherously.

God accused the children of Israel of dealing treacherously with the wife of their youth by divorcing her for a strange woman. They did not ask God about this new union because they knew it was forbidden. Israel simply disobeyed the laws and commandments in pursuit of their own will, actions, and lusts. Did he not make them as one? The question is referring to Genesis and the original intent of marriage. Ordained by God, marriage was intended to be a lasting covenant between two people whom God joined. God's purpose for marriage was not just for the children of Israel. It is for every believer.

Many marriages and subsequent divorces are the result of people not asking God to give them a mate. When we don't consult God, we make bad choices in relationships. Often, the decisions made in the natural do not consider the spiritual aspect of the marriage.

Let's look at an example of a divinely directed choice of a mate for Isaac. When Abraham was getting old, he wanted to make sure that his son, Isaac, had a wife. It could not be just any woman. Abraham followed the commandment of the Lord. Therefore, he made his servant swear that he would obey God's will. Genesis 24:3-4 states:

3 And I will make thee swear by the LORD, the God of heaven, and the God of the earth, that thou shalt not take a wife unto my son of the daughters of the Canaanites, among whom I dwell:
4 But thou shalt go unto my country, and to my kindred, and take a wife unto my son Isaac.

There could be no strange woman for Isaac. Abraham was obedient to what the Lord commanded in selecting a wife. He was so confident in the Lord that he told the servant that God would send his angel before him to assist him. Divinely selected by God, Rebekah and her family agreed with the servant when he relayed the message. Genesis 24 states:

51 Behold, Rebekah is before thee, take her, and go, and let her be thy master's son's wife, as the LORD hath spoken.
67 And Isaac brought her into his mother Sarah's tent, and took Rebekah, and she became his wife; and he loved her: and Isaac was comforted after his mother's death.

From the seed of Isaac came Jacob and from this relationship came a holy nation. God joined them, and there was no broken covenant. Israel was rich in heritage but poor in obedience. At every opportunity, Israel disobeyed the commandments of God regarding the people of other lands. They insisted on trespassing the commandments. Ezra 9:1-2 describes their actions:

9:1 Now when these things were done, the princes came to me, saying, The people of Israel, and the priests, and the Levites, have not separated themselves from the people of the lands, doing according to their abominations, even of the Canaanites, the Hittites, the Perizzites, the Jebusites, the Ammonites, the Moabites, the Egyptians, and the Amorites.
2 For they have taken of their daughters for themselves, and for their sons: so that the holy seed have mingled themselves with the people of those lands: yea, the hand of the princes and rulers hath been chief in this trespass.

Ezra describes the unholy union with the women of a strange land as mingling the holy seed with the people of the land. If the children of Israel continued polluting themselves by marrying those from strange nations, how would Jesus descend from Israel as a godly seed? Israel's marriage to strange gods rather than marriage to a Holy God would contaminate the bloodline of Jesus. There had to be a solution.

Ezra prayed for the sin committed by Israel for this great transgression. Israel repented and offered a solution to the sin, divorce. Ezra 10:2-3 explains what took place.

2 And Shechaniah the son of Jehiel, one of the sons of Elam, answered and said unto Ezra, We have trespassed against our God, and have taken strange wives of the people of the land: yet now there is hope in Israel concerning this thing.

3 Now therefore let us make a covenant with our God to put away all the wives, and such as are born of them, according to the counsel of my lord, and of those that tremble at the commandment of our God; and let it be done according to the law.

The decision made by the people to put away the strange wives and children halted the judgment against them. The yoke represented sin, separation, and bondage. It drew back God's face from them because He was not pleased with their behavior. It allowed sin to reign, and it was spiritual adultery. Adultery is betrayal and violation of the covenant of marriage, a broken yoke, and a violation of a decree. Divorce ends a relationship. It denotes a broken covenant, a disannulment, and a severed relationship. It is putting away of the selected into the streets.

The Pharisees were a stickler for the law, and they knew the answer to the question on divorce. They asked Jesus to get a ruling on the matter. Jesus referred them to Moses and the law. He reaffirmed God's purpose for marriage and their need for a holy yoke. Matthew 19 states:

3 The Pharisees also came unto him, tempting him, and saying unto him, Is it lawful for a man to put away his wife for every cause?
4 And he answered and said unto them, Have ye not read, that he which made them at the beginning made them male and female,
5 And said, For this cause shall a man leave father and mother, and shall cleave to his wife: and they twain shall be one flesh?
6 Wherefore they are no more twain, but one flesh. What therefore God hath joined together, let not man put asunder.
7 They say unto him, Why did Moses then command to give a writing of divorcement, and to put her away?

26

8 He saith unto them, Moses because of the hardness of your hearts suffered you to put away your wives: but from the beginning it was not so.

First, the Pharisees asked Jesus *"Is it lawful for a man to put away his wife for every cause?"* To justify their position on divorce they wanted Jesus to give a ruling on the matter. The clue to the question was for "every cause." Their attitude was they could divorce based on any reason or circumstances. If they did not want the person, he or she was gone. Jesus wanted them to consider their actions so He restated the original intent of marriage. They still questioned Jesus' answer because Moses allowed them to divorce. Therefore, there was still controversy over whom to believe, Moses or Jesus. He further explained Moses permitted them to divorce because their actions and attitudes were callous. They did not care about the spouse, and they were determined to divorce them.

Moses made a law to protect the person who was put away. Because of the teachings on adultery, the Pharisees were very familiar with the law. They were also familiar with the Word and how throughout history, Israel committed adultery with strange gods of strange lands. Jesus related this teaching to their hardness and callous reasons for divorce. He said in Matthew 19:9:

9 And I say unto you, Whosoever shall put away his wife, except it be for fornication, and shall marry another, committeth adultery: and whoso marrieth her which is put away doth commit adultery.

The action of divorce resulting from the immoral behavior of the wife was an acknowledgment of the sin. As stated in Deuteronomy 24:1, *"When a man hath taken a wife, and married her, and it come to pass that she find no favour in his eyes, because he hath found some uncleanness in her: then let him write her a bill of divorcement, and give it in her hand, and send her out of his house."*

The husband could put the wife away because he found some uncleanness in her. From the original intent of divorce; there was a sin, uncleanness. Adultery came into play when Israel began to establish what was unclean. They felt it meant any cause. Therefore, they betrayed their former wife to establish a relationship with someone else. Mark 10:11-12 further clarifies this teaching:

11 And he saith unto them, Whosoever shall put away his wife, and marry another, committeth adultery against her. 12 And if a woman shall put away her husband, and be married to another, she committeth adultery.

The value derived from the teaching is that divorce for "any cause" caused the man or woman to commit adultery against his wife or husband. Putting away caused (forced) the injured party to commit adultery against his or her will. Matthew 5:32: states, *"But I say unto you, That whosoever shall put away his wife, saving for the cause of fornication, causeth her to commit adultery: and whosoever shall marry her that is divorced committeth adultery."*

Adultery is a work of the flesh. It is a selfish act conceived in lust. Lust begins in the heart and manifests in the flesh. Adultery is a sin of the heart. The Bible often speaks of adultery as it relates to the unfaithfulness and betrayal of Israel towards God and His commandments. Therefore, God understands fully the emotional strain adultery has on relationships and marriage. It is a perversion of the spiritual intent of matrimony.

28

It is God's will for people to marry. It is God's will for believers to select a mate of an equal yoke. The problem with divorce today is not necessarily the husband or the wife. The problem is with choices. When choices are not correct, the foundation is unstable. Second Corinthians 6:14-16 teaches:

14 Be ye not unequally yoked together with unbelievers: for what fellowship hath righteousness with unrighteousness? And what communion hath light with darkness?
15 And what concord hath Christ with Belial? or what part hath he that believeth with an infidel?
16 And what agreement hath the temple of God with idols? for ye are the temple of the living God; as God hath said, I will dwell in them, and walk in them; and I will be their God, and they shall be my people.

The passage reminds us that we are the temple (dwelling place) of God. It is important that we select a mate by the Spirit and not our flesh. There is nothing wrong with the scriptures or Jesus' teachings. Both provide a blueprint for us to follow on how to live and love unconditionally. For many, loving people unconditionally is a strange concept. We offend, judge, condemn and hurt others through our beliefs, actions, and heresy (errors in teaching). Let us end the discrimination surrounding divorce and offer love.

To the Divorced

Do not allow the poison of men or women hold you in bondage. Let go of the anger and the grief you feel because of divorce. Trust in the loving kindness of Jesus and His grace. If you are tormented and bound by guilt, it is not from Jesus. He forgives every unrighteous act. He gave His life so you could be free. Jesus does not judge

29

people nor condemn you. His kindness can reach you. There are no boundaries.

I want to end this chapter in revelation from the Holy Ghost. It is plain to me that the problem is in not asking God for a spouse or if you do ask, you do not wait to hear His response. Sometimes we hear what we want to hear. If a divorced believer admits it, there were warnings at the beginning or during the courtship stages. However, the person did not listen or adhere to the leading of the Holy Ghost. Remember, divorce or marriage becomes a choice.

The Holy Ghost gave to me this statement for the believer:

Why be in bondage? You haven't asked me. You feared you would be denied. So, you go and align with a yoke without me and get in trouble. I did not join it. When it is broken, you go a whoring to select the next person, then that yoke is broken (adultery begins). There is a better solution. Keep yourself from unholy yokes. Avoid the trouble. Repent of the anger of being out of my will. Concentrate on a holy yoke or no yoke. The only failure seen in divorce is in your choices. They were not of me. That is your bondage. Now, receive a good report. I will show you how to live when I join you. The door is open. What is in your heart, I will hear? I will heal you with peace. Now live!

CHAPTER THREE
GENESIS-A NEW BEGINNING

Call unto me, and I will answer thee, and show thee great and mighty things, which thou knowest not. Jeremiah 33:3

Inside of our brokenness and despair, God wants to give us a fresh start. I am not perfect, you are not perfect, and life is not perfect. The only perfect one is the Father, Son, and the Holy Ghost. I believe, for healing and cleansing to take place, we must accept ourselves with all our imperfections even as God accepts us.

In Chapter 1, I shared my story of God's love, mercy, and deliverance as He walked me through separation and then through a divorce. All I want anyone to see and understand is how a loving God the Father cares and loves His children. How we walk out our destiny depends on how we receive and accept His love and grace. As for me, I purpose to live life. I was too long in survival mode not to value and appreciate this wonderful place of grace and abundant life. The journey begins by accepting the gift of a fresh start.

The Cleansing and Healing Process

Removing ourselves from a bad situation is only the beginning of the journey to recovery, being healed, delivered, and set free. After God has done His part, we must begin to regroup. Often, this requires soul searching, forgiveness of the one who caused the pain, and forgiveness of oneself. A new job, a new apartment, new people but you ask, what is missing? The answer is a new you.

Moving to a new location does not solve all your problems because you take the old you with you. The cleansing and healing begin in the heart. David said it best in Psalms 51:10 *"Create in me a clean heart, O God; and renew a right spirit within me."* Our prayer to God is for a clean heart, free from the clutter of the previous years of our life that was full of agony, grief, sorrow, and anguish of soul. We need an extreme makeover for the spirit, soul, mind, and body. For this to take place, we need to let some things go. Isaiah 43:18-19 reminds us to "*Remember ye not the former things, neither consider the things of old. Behold, I will do a new thing; now it shall spring forth; shall ye not know it? I will make a way in the wilderness, and rivers in the desert."* Do not look back; keep moving forward. God made a way for you. He heard your cry for help.

The Bible plainly shows us, time after time, that when those in distress called upon the Lord, He answered. For example, the leper in Matthew 8:2-3 received his healing when he called upon Jesus. By crying out, the leper made his request known. He expressed a need and Jesus met the need. *"And, behold, there came a leper and worshipped him, saying, Lord, if thou wilt, thou canst make me clean. And Jesus put forth his hand, and touched him, saying, I will; be thou clean. And immediately his leprosy was cleansed."*

The leper, like many people, posed the same question, "if thou wilt." We never doubt that Jesus can heal us, but we always question, if he will heal. Therefore, he said, *"if thou wilt, thou canst make me clean."* Jesus did not waste any time pondering whether to touch the leper or not. Technically, the Levitical law had rules and regulations

32

regarding leprosy. The man was legally and ceremonially unclean. However, Jesus, the healer, is greater than the law. He demonstrated through that touch that compassion and mercy took precedence over the law. The touch spoke volumes. I believe it said, I love you, I forgive you, I care, you matter, and you're healed. Let Jesus touch you today and take away the hurt and pain. He wants to put forth his hand to heal you and say, "I will be thou clean."

What is the key to receiving healing? Let's examine what elements were present for the leper to receive his healing. First, he came and worshiped Jesus. He humbled himself and bowed down before Jesus in total submission to His power and grace. This leper understood and reverenced the awesome power that was in his midst to heal. He did not come in his strength or self worth. He recognized Jesus as the only person who could save and deliver him. He needed a miracle; yet, he took the time to worship Jesus.

To worship Jesus, you must come into his presence with total respect, reverence, and honor for the King. Do not just rush into the throne room with a list of petitions without acknowledging God's holiness or deity. When you awake in the morning, do you greet the people in your house with, good morning? Likewise, when you come into God's house, greet Him.

During that time of worship, forget about yourself and recognize that you are in the presence of the Almighty God. Begin to love and adore Him just for who He is and not for what you can get. Take time to reverence and give thanks. Remind God of His greatness and thank Jesus for what He has done. I always read or quote passages to the Lord to remind Him of the covenant and that He is not a respecter of persons. I stand for my miracle based on the Word and you can too.

Tell Jesus about the situation and get results. On another occasion, two blind men had heard about Jesus and His ability to heal. Their plea was simple, *"Thou son of David, have mercy on us" (Mt. 9:27)*. Mercy goes hand in hand with repentance. The Jews believed if someone had something wrong with them that someone in their family had sinned and a curse had passed down. The blind men asked for mercy. Justice gives you what you deserve; mercy gives you what you do not deserve. Have compassion on us, forgive us and heal was the heart cry of those blind men. Jesus replied, *"Believe ye that I am able to do this? They said unto him, Yea, Lord. Then touched he their eyes, saying, According to your faith be it unto you" (Mt. 9:28-29)*.

According to your faith is a powerful statement. You have to believe that Jesus will heal you and forgive you. Often, we want to put the entire burden on Jesus or other people for healing. You must contribute to the process by believing, with confidence, that He is able and willing to heal you. It is not a question of whether Jesus will heal; it is a question of do you believe he will heal you.

Where Is Your Faith?

From the two examples, we learn the key to receiving anything from Christ is faith. Faith simply believes God is able. Faith requires us to trust in God's ability to get the job done, not in ourselves. You place your confidence in the Messiah, the Savior, the Healer, the Prince of Peace, and the King of Kings. It does not matter what the circumstances are, your deliverance will surely come when you reach out to Jesus, the Savior, to save you.

Matthew 14:22-33 illustrates how Jesus is willing to save people. When Peter needed the Savior, He was right there. He saw Jesus walking on water, and he said, *"Lord, if it be thou, bid me come unto thee on the water" (vs. 27)*. Of course, Jesus told Peter to come because He did not want to stifle Peter's confidence nor willingness to experience this miracle. Encouraging Peter, Jesus said, *"Come" (vs. 29)*. Peter began to walk on water just like Jesus. However, for a fleeting moment, he took his eyes off the Savior, looked on the circumstances surrounding him, and allowed fear to grip him. Peter began to sink.

As Peter began to sink, he cried, *"Lord, save me" (vs. 30)*. Peter recognized he was in a dilemma; he needed help from the Savior. *"And immediately Jesus stretched forth his hand, and caught him, and said unto him, O thou of little faith, wherefore didst thou doubt?" (vs. 31)*. Jesus did not let Peter drown; he reached for Peter and lifted him up to safety. After Jesus had taken care of the immediate situation, drowning, he delved into a much more serious situation, the question of Peter's faith.

Peter began in faith and ended in fear. Faith allowed him to make the bold step. However, fear caused him to sink. In many situations, people begin in faith. When it takes too long to accomplish a task or receive an answer from God, doubt, unbelief, and fear enter. What caused Peter to doubt?

The same question Jesus asked Peter is the same question he asks us today. Why did you doubt? Why did you fear? Fear is the opposite of faith. Fear tells you what you don't have and what you can't do. Faith responds with positive words grounded and rooted in a powerful person, Jesus, and an awesome testimony, the Word of God. You have the faith necessary to believe God for healing, deliverance, finances, salvation, and all your needs. God has given to everyone the measure of faith (Rom. 12:3). So, do not fear, exercise your faith. *"For God hath not given us the spirit of fear; but of power, and of love, and of a sound mind," (2 Tim. 1:7).* Stir up the faith that is on the inside of you to receive from God the answer to your prayer.

God Answers Prayer

I love to pray! In prayer, I talk to God, and I expect Him to talk to me. From the scriptures, I have learned how to get results. Faith is the key to releasing a prayer. You have to trust and believe that God answers. Hezekiah had a wonderful testimony about the power of prayer. Every time I read about Hezekiah, I encourage myself in the Lord. The message of prayer, mercy, and deliverance he received from God is inspiring.

Isaiah 38:1-3 records Hezekiah's story:

1 In those days was Hezekiah sick unto death. And Isaiah the prophet the son of Amoz came unto him, and said unto him, Thus saith the LORD, Set thine house in order: for thou shalt die, and not live.
2 Then Hezekiah turned his face toward the wall, and prayed unto the LORD,
3 And said, Remember now, O LORD, I beseech thee, how I have walked before thee in truth and with a perfect heart, and have done that which is good in thy sight. And Hezekiah wept sore.

The prophet, Isaiah, told Hezekiah to set his house in order because he was going to die. First, you must understand that the prophet was speaking a message straight from the throne of God, "*Set thine house in order*" *(vs. 1).* God gave Hezekiah an opportunity to straighten things out or set things in order before leaving the earth. However, Hezekiah was not ready to die. Instead of preparing for death, he made a petition to God for life. That took courage!

In his distress, Hezekiah turned his face to the wall and shut out the words of Isaiah, his surroundings, his family, friends, and kingdom. At that point, in his life, Hezekiah's position, stature, possessions, and world estate did not matter. Faced with a proclamation of death, Hezekiah cried out to God with a request for life. He did not accept the report of death without first petitioning the source of life. In his supplication, he prayed earnestly, calling upon God to remember his walk.

We need to follow Hezekiah's example and ask God for life. Too many times, we accept a bad report from a doctor, lawyer, officials, etc., and we give up too soon. Like Hezekiah, so many of us have had a similar report from a doctor. I remember I was bleeding profusely for months because of fibroid tumors. I had been in and out of the hospital with no change. Therefore, I made an appointment to go back to Jonesboro, Arkansas, 50 miles away, to my previous gynecologist for help. Several years before the complications, the doctor had performed tubal ligation surgery.

You can have a wonderful time of prayer traveling 50 miles. As I approached the stop light just before his office, the Holy Spirit began to pray radically for me the answer. He knew I was going to receive a bad report and He did not want me to accept it. The answer the Holy Ghost gave me was, "NO." When the doctor examined me, he decided to try another medication. He stated, "Since you don't want any more children if this medicine does not help, I will perform a hysterectomy." The answer was "NO." Regardless of whether the medicine worked or not, God told me no to a hysterectomy. It does not hurt to get a second opinion. Unfortunately, some doctors believe the only solution is surgery. Dr. Jesus had another solution.

During this walk of faith, I prayed for direction. I try not to make a move now without the Lord, and I pray about everything even the smallest, simplest thing. You may say, why would anyone do that? I am glad you asked. I show God the utmost respect by involving Him in my life choices on the front end rather than wait until I am in a crisis and need Him to rescue me. You see, I want the Lord involved in every aspect of my life. Therefore, I talk to Him. I cannot take credit like this was an original idea. I learned this from David's relationship with God. What I observed, while reading the Bible is that David made inquiring of the Lord his lifestyle. Below are scriptural references to consider:

Then David enquired of the Lord yet again. And the Lord answered him and said, Arise, go down to Keilah; for I will deliver the Philistines into thine hand (1 Sam. 23:4).

And David enquired at the Lord, saying, Shall I pursue after this troop? shall I overtake them? And he answered him, Pursue: for thou shalt surely overtake them, and without fail recover all (1 Sam. 30:8).

And it came to pass after this, that David enquired of the Lord, saying, Shall I go up into any of the cities of Judah? And the Lord said unto him, Go up. And David said, Whither shall I go up? And he said, Unto Hebron (2 Sam. 2:1).

And David enquired of the Lord, saying, Shall I go up to the Philistines? wilt thou deliver them into mine hand?

And the Lord said unto David, Go up: for I will doubtless deliver the Philistines into thine hand (2 Sam. 15:19).

And when David enquired of the Lord, he said, Thou shalt not go up; but fetch a compass behind them, and come upon them over against the mulberry trees (2 Sam. 5:23).

Following David's pattern has helped me tremendously along life's path. I understand from David that asking God about everything has saved his life on numerous occasions. Think about this concept. When you have a broken part or an appliance, you take it back to the manufacturer for repairs. Well, God made us so who better can diagnose and heal what is wrong than the one who made us. So, I ask Him. When you do this, you have to trust Him and believe that you hear Him. Do not bother to involve God if you do not intend to obey Him when He gives an answer that you do not like. It is all about faith and trust.

A walk of faith requires you to trust the Word of God and stand on the Word. In addition to seeking another doctor's opinion for the medical condition I mentioned earlier, I fed my body with the Word. The scripture that I rely on is Isaiah 53:5, "with his *stripes we are healed.*" I meditated on the Word. The next doctor I saw did not believe that the solution to this problem was a hysterectomy. She scraped the walls, prescribed stronger medication, and required iron pills. With each pill I took, I prayed over it, quoted the scriptures, and said, "in Jesus name, the power is in your name." One particular morning, as I reached for the pill, the Holy Ghost said, "you don't need those anymore." I stopped the medication and praised God. I am still healed today and no surgery.

Now let me warn you. When you stand by faith for your healing, and God heals you, the devil will come to try to steal your healing by duplicating the symptoms. Often, people say, I thought God healed me. The enemy of your faith is trying to get you to doubt God. Do not believe the hype. Just continue to stand on the Word and quote the same scriptures you stood on to get the healing. I remember when I was under stress in the midst of the divorce; I had one bout with the symptoms of bleeding returning. I recognized the hand of the enemy and refused to fall for that trick because God healed me. I had just moved to Florida; I did not know any doctors. Furthermore, I did not even know my way around the city. I relied on the Savior, increased my reading, meditated on healing scriptures, sang songs on healing, and kept confessing God's Word. The symptoms left and did not return. The devil will try you so do not fret or have fear concerning it. Stand faithful trusting God's Word more than what you see or how you feel. For we walk by faith, not by sight as stated in 2 Cor. 5:7.

What is going on in your life? Perhaps, doctors have given you only a few months to live, or you have given yourself only a few days to live. You could be contemplating suicide right now. You have a choice today to live or die. Are you going to believe God for your life or give up on life? I always remind myself of the mercy God bestowed on King Hezekiah when he was facing death. Remember, Hezekiah did not accept the message and he got results. Isaiah 38:4-5 records the incident. *"Then came the word of the LORD to Isaiah, saying, 5Go, and say to Hezekiah, Thus saith the LORD, the God of David thy father, I have heard thy prayer, I have seen thy tears: behold, I will add unto thy days fifteen years."*

God said I have heard your prayers. It is a great feeling to know that God hears our prayer. Sometimes we are too quick to say, I don't think God hears me. When you do that, you are giving way to doubt and unbelief. If you have said negative words like this, repent. Ask God to forgive the words of your mouth. Begin to cancel out the negative words by quoting the positive words found in the Bible. Find a scripture that relates to your situation and stand upon the Word to get results.

Peace in the Midst of Trials and Tribulations

Trusting God was easy for the three Hebrew men, Shadrach, Meshach, and Abednego. They loved God and stood on their faith that God was able to deliver them from adversity. When King Nebuchadnezzar made a decree that all would bow and worship the golden image, the three Hebrew men would not bow. The king declared that anyone not bowing to the statue would be thrown into the fiery furnace. However, the Hebrew men stood firm and answered King Nebuchadnezzar, *"If it be so, our God whom we serve is able to deliver us from the burning fiery furnace, and he will deliver us out of thine hand, O king" (Dan. 3:17).* All they determined to know concerning the matter at hand was that God was able to deliver them. We must hold fast to that same conviction; God can deliver. Your circumstances do not move God. Whatever it takes, you must have faith that God can and will deliver you.

The three Hebrew men were bound in their clothing and cast into the midst of the burning fiery furnace. The flames slew the men who threw them in the fire. However, the flame did not consume Shadrach, Meshach, and Abednego. When Nebuchadnezzar pierced into the flame, he stated, *"Lo, I see four men loose, walking in the midst of the fire, and they have no hurt; and the form of the fourth is like the Son of God" (Dan. 3:25).* The flames could not touch them because God was in control. If it

41

requires Him to send an angel to help you, He will do it. Again, whatever it takes, God can deliver you. God heard the words of the Hebrew men who trusted in Him; He hearkened unto their words. He delivered them from adversity and gave them peace in the midst of their trial.

Do not take it personally when adversity bombards you. *"Beloved, think it not strange concerning the fiery trial which is to try you, as though some strange thing happened unto you" (1 Pet. 4:12).* We tend to think whatever we are going through is unique. It is not! Do you know what a trial is? The word, fiery trial, in the Greek means, purosis, a calamity or burning (Strong's Talking Greek & Hebrew Dictionary, 2017). The trial is not against you nor is adversity seeking you out. The enemy tries the Word of the Lord, not YOU!

Psalms 18:30 states, *"As for God, his way is perfect: the word of the LORD is tried: he is a buckler to all those that trust in him."* How is the word of the Lord tried? When pressure, circumstances, affliction, oppression, financial difficulty, and health issues occur, the adversary questions your faith and tries to make you doubt God. He wants to see if you will stand in faith, trusting the Word or crumble under pressure. If you crumble, the adversary wins. However, if you stand on the Word, trust God, and wait patiently, you will obtain great results.

What did Jesus mean when he said *"in the world, ye shall have tribulations" (Jn. 16:33)?* Tribulation, from the Greek word thlipsis, means pressure (lit. or fig.): -afflicted, (-tion), anguish, burdened, persecution, tribulation, and trouble (Strong's Talking Greek & Hebrew Dictionary, 2017). When you are going through trials and tribulation, you are under such pressure and affliction that the trials cause anguish of soul. Remember Jesus warned us that we would have tribulation. The good news is that He has overcome the world with all tribulations hindering our walk in total victory.

Persecutions, afflictions, anguish, and adversity are the tools the devil uses to war against people. We are warned to *"Be sober, be vigilant; because your adversary the devil, as a roaring lion, walketh about, seeking whom he may devour: Whom resist stedfast in the faith, knowing that the same afflictions are accomplished in your brethren that are in the world" (1 Pet. 5:8-9).* Jesus defeated the devil; so, you are not in a fight with him. You are only fighting the good fight of faith. By faith, all you need to do is walk in the revelation of the Word and Jesus' accomplishment. The devil's tactics are always the same. However, if you resist the devil, he will flee (Jas. 4:7). If you believe, you will have victory over the enemy every time.

Most people want to believe that Jesus is able. However, they are not sure He will do what they ask. Rest assured what He has done for others He will do for you; only believe and trust Him. Sometimes it is good to remind God of His promises. A good promise to stand on is Psalms 91:15-16 that states, *"He shall call upon me, and I will answer him: I will be with him in trouble; I will deliver him, and honour him. 16 With long life will I satisfy him, and show him my salvation."* Notice the Word again. How many times did God state, I will? There are several things God promised He would do in Psalms 91. Rest assured God keeps His promises. Numbers 23:19 reminds us that *"God is not a man, that he should lie; neither the son of man, that he should repent: hath he said, and shall he not do it? or hath he spoken, and shall he not make it good."* God is not man; He is sovereign God-all powerful and all knowing.

In Jeremiah 29:12-13, we are encouraged to call upon the Lord and ask for help. *"Then shall ye call upon me, and ye shall go and pray unto me, and I will hearken unto you. And ye shall seek me, and find me, when ye shall search for me with all your heart."* If you ever want to know the will of God, read the Word. It is not a mystery what God is willing and able to do if you seek Him.

Through faith, you can receive any promise given in His Word. God will never tell you to ask for something He is not willing or cannot give. Confidence in God's ability to deliver is born from a relationship. It is hard to trust someone you do not know. Take time to find out about the Father and Jesus and allow your trust to grow. Remember, He is always there for you. Whatever you need to obtain a breakthrough, to overcome the wiles of the devil, or to live a victorious life, He has already provided. Help is only a call away.

"The LORD hear thee in the day of trouble; the name of the God of Jacob defend thee; Send thee help from the sanctuary, and strengthen thee out of Zion" (Ps. 20:1-2).

CHAPTER FOUR
ALL MY HELP

When I moved to Florida in 1995, I knew God had more for me to do. Before leaving Arkansas, He told me I was going to start a church. From 1995 to 1999, I learned the lay of the land and worked in another church to help the pastor with his university. I became acclimated to the culture and complexity of a metropolitan area. I was excited about the work God had for me.

When I began to pastor a church in 1999, I learned so much about people and the oppressing force in their lives. So many Christians and people, in general, are in Egypt today, afflicted, persecuted, and bound. Egypt represents bondage! The word Egypt, in Hebrew, is matsowr. It means something is hemming in, i.e., a mound, a siege, distress; or a fastness: -besieged, bulwark, defence, fenced, fortress, siege, strong (hold), and tower (Strong's Greek & Hebrew Dictionary, 2017). Do any of these adjectives describe what you are feeling today? Does a stronghold have you chained? Do you feel distressed or overcome by someone or something? If your reply is yes, you are in a spiritual Egypt, a place of bondage. God does not want you enslaved by a yoke of bondage any longer. He wants us to *"Stand fast therefore in the liberty wherewith Christ hath made us free, and be not entangled again with the yoke of bondage"* (Gal. 5:1).

What is a yoke of bondage? Imagine two oxen connected by a yoke, which is a harness. The yoke binds the two animals together so they can pull a load. Now picture yourself connected by a yoke to any addiction, person, or thing that has you bound. With a yoke, you are at the mercy of the other animal or in your case the bondage. Because a yoke connects you, you cannot go where you want to go or do what you want to do. The yoke controls you because you and the thing that you are tied to must move together.

When you are yoked or bound, that yoke enslaves you. Bondage (slavery) is a spirit; it locks you up and controls your every move. The spirit chains you to a situation, addiction, or a person.

Even though you can identify what has you bound, it is important not to be caught up in the "why me" syndrome. You are not a victim. Having a pity party is dangerous. You will open the door for more persecutions. The Bible states: *"Submit yourselves therefore to God. Resist the devil, and he will flee from you" (Jas 4:7)*. You have the strategy for overcoming strongholds or things that hinder your progress in life. God is here to help you be victorious.

What has you bound today? I have selected some topics and solutions based on the scripture, situations, or people I encountered over the years. I hope the examples and solutions will help you.

Bound by Fear

Throughout the scriptures, God constantly reminds us to "Fear not." It is a commandment for you not to fear. Obey the commandment and take authority over the fear. Fear is the opposite of faith. If you are walking in fear, there is no faith. *"For ye have not received the spirit of bondage again to fear; but ye have received the Spirit of adoption, whereby we cry, Abba, Father" (Rom. 8:15)*. You did not receive this spirit of bondage to fear from God; so, it had to come from somewhere. Obviously, it came straight from the enemy, Satan. Jesus defeated Satan and destroyed all his works. The only power or stronghold the devil has over you is the power that you release to him.

Fear is an evil, wicked spirit that comes straight from the pit of hell. It is a spirit that grips the heart and torments the soul. When fear binds, you begin to alter what you normally would do because you are afraid. If you are worried about something, your expectations are controlled by fear. If you expect someone to attack, kill, or rob you, anxiousness and apprehension occur. Fear draws to you exactly what you do not want to happen. Let me give you an example from the Word as recorded in Job chapters 1-3. Job continually offered sacrifices for his sons and daughters. They would have a feast and Job was afraid that during their drinking and feasting, they might curse God in their hearts. He wanted to offer a sacrifice to appease God or atone for their sins just in case it happened.

One day Job received a report. The messenger told Job that his sons and daughters were eating and drinking wine in their eldest brother's house and a great wind from the wilderness smote the four corners of the house. It fell upon the young men, and they died. As Job thought about the series of mishaps and tragedies that befell him that day, he stated, *"For the thing which I greatly feared is come upon me, and that which I was afraid of is come unto me" (Job 3:25)*. He took responsibility for his thoughts and fear. Job expected bad things to happen and they did because he operated in fear. Do not expect the worse; you will get the worse. Fear is like a magnet; it draws to you what you do not want to happen. Place your hope and trust in God. Learn from Job's experience.

To get different results, you must change your expectation level and the words that you speak. Proverbs 18:21 states, *"Death and life are in the power of the tongue: and they that love it shall eat the fruit thereof."* When you speak, the words spoken will be either life or death. The words cause one of those agents, death or life, to go to work for you. Will you speak death or life today?

Often, without thinking, we make statements like that scared me to death. Do you see the death connection? Some people become so gripped by fear; they have a heart attack. Even the Word states in Luke 21:25, *"Men's hearts failing them for fear."* If you had a fear of snakes, heights, spiders, or being in closed spaces that would be a common fear. Some people even seek psychiatric help to overcome fears. You must understand that you are dealing with a spirit and not something that medication can treat.

In addition to the common fears, there are the more subtle, deadly fears. What are they? They are the stronger, deep-rooted emotional fears such as fear of rejection, fear of failure, fear of the past, or fear of death. These fears are soul connected to a person or a specific incident. You may have heard the term soul ties. The best explanation from the Word I can give you on soul ties comes from the relationship Jonathan had with David. Samuel stated, *"that the soul of Jonathan was knit with the soul of David, and Jonathan loved him as his own soul"* (1 Sam. 18:1). The key to this explanation is the word knit, which means bound or joined. As friends, Jonathan and David were bound together by friendship, fellowship, and relationship. They were soul connected.

When fears are soul connected, bound together by relationship or association with someone or something, they are harder to break. You have to get to the root of the fear and drive it out. Can you identify what caused your

48

fear? Was it abuse, divorce, betrayal, abandonment, a sudden death, or was it a mistake or a bad decision that had great repercussions? Is your past haunting you? If you try to make a decision or move forward in life and a glimpse of your past or hurt arises, then you are immobilized by that fear.

Sometimes even judgment becomes clouded by fear. Individuals are afraid to love because someone hurt them. All other relationships become bound by the fear of a previous relationship. Some even declare I will never love again. However, God's Word assures us we are not to fear love. *"There is no fear in love; but perfect love casteth out fear: because fear hath torment. He that feareth is not made perfect in love" (1 John 4:18)*. Perfect, mature love is born of the spirit. The Word tells us that love is a fruit of the spirit. It is the nature and character of God. Usually, love is described sensually based on how it makes one feel. We think we are in love because we get weak in the knees or get goosebumps when he or she walks in the room. However, that love requires us to do something constantly to maintain those experiences. When you love someone, it should be as natural as breathing. Since love represents the very essence and character of God, love is from the heart. Do not fear relationships.

Besides relationships, another area that causes great fear is death. When people have a fear of dying, they are uncertain about where they are going after death. Paul answered the question when he taught the church at Corinth about the death of those that were born again. In 2 Corinthians 5:6-8, he states, *"Therefore we are always confident, knowing that, whilst we are at home in the body, we are absent from the Lord: 7(For we walk by faith, not by sight:) 8 We are confident, I say, and willing rather to be absent from the body, and to be present with*

49

the Lord." According to the Word, when a Christian dies, he is immediately in the presence of the Lord. As Paul wrestled with the decision to leave the earth, he told the church at Philippi that he had a decision to make. *"For I am in a strait betwixt two, having a desire to depart, and to be with Christ; which is far better: Nevertheless to abide in the flesh is more needful for you" (Phil. 1:23-24).* In that same moment of contemplation, Paul made a quality decision to stay and further assist the church. Paul chose not to die!

Jesus also knew people had a fear of the unknown. He settled the issue concerning death. Hebrews 2:14-15 states, *"Forasmuch then as the children are partakers of flesh and blood, he also himself likewise took part of the same; that through death he might destroy him that had the power of death, that is, the devil; 15 And deliver them who through fear of death were all their lifetime subject to bondage."* Verse 15 states that people were all their lifetime subject to bondage because of the fear of death. They were slaves to that fear. Through death, Jesus destroyed the one who had power over death by tasting death for us. In Revelations 1:18, Jesus states, *"I am he that liveth, and was dead; and, behold, I am alive for evermore, Amen; and have the keys of hell and of death."* Jesus settled the issue. He unlocked the mystery surrounding death by experiencing death. Jesus traded the death sentence for a life sentence of eternal life with Him.

Furthermore, Jesus stated in Matthew 16:19, *"And I will give unto thee the keys of the kingdom of heaven: and whatsoever thou shalt bind on earth shall be bound in heaven: and whatsoever thou shalt loose on earth shall be loosed in heaven."* You have the keys, and you are in the driver's seat. The keys you have are not ordinary keys. You have a responsibility and choices to make because what you bind on earth you bind in the heavens.

50

Likewise, what you loose on earth you loose in heaven. The choice is yours.

In Christ, you are free from sin and death. You do not have to fear death any longer. Jesus experienced death for you so that He could deliver you from that bondage of fear. Jesus defeated the devil and gave you the power to tread on the enemy. You have nothing to fear; you have the power to bind fear. Jesus said, *"Behold, I give unto you power to tread on serpents and scorpions, and over all the power of the enemy: and nothing shall by any means hurt you. 20 Notwithstanding in this rejoice not, that the spirits are subject unto you; but rather rejoice, because your names are written in heaven" (Lk. 10:19-20).* As one who believes in Jesus Christ as your Savior, you have power over all the power of the enemy. Exercise your rights as a believer. Find a scripture to stand on and confess the scripture, not your fears. Stand fast in such great liberty and authority delegated to you.

Take back everything the enemy has stolen from you! Regain your dignity and your freedom. Do not be ashamed. At some point in our lives, fear gripped us. The solution to any fear is Jesus; He wants to set you free from worry and fear. God has given us the power to overcome fear. If fear tries to grip you, quote the words of 2 Timothy 1:7, *"For God hath not given us the spirit of fear, but of power, and of love, and of a sound mind."* You must make a quality decision to break the power of fear over your life. Take authority over the torment of fear now. Speak to the fear and declare your liberty. Say: I bind fear, in the name of Jesus. Fear, I denounce you and your power over me is broken according to the Word of God. I command this spirit of fear to leave me NOW, in the name of Jesus! Memorize and quote this scripture every time fear tries to torment you. *"For God hath not given us the spirit of fear, but of power, and of love, and of a sound mind"* (2 Tim. 1:7). Let the scripture be your confession of faith. Remember, "FEAR NOT."

The Deadly Bondage of Control

Many people are not imprisoned physically but mentally. There is a force operating in them, and it is called control. What is control? Control is the power to manage, direct, or dominate (Dictionary.com, 2017). The force is active in the land, and it has to do with dominance. Where did control begin? Genesis 1: 27-28 states:

"So God created man in his own image, in the image of God created he him; male and female created he them. 28 And God blessed them, and God said unto them, Be fruitful, and multiply, and replenish the earth, and subdue it: and have dominion over the fish of the sea, and over the fowl of the air, and over every living thing that moveth upon the earth."

Adam and Eve had instructions to replenish the earth and subdue it. Subdue here is taken from the Hebrew word, kabash, which means to tread down; hence, to disregard; to conquer, subjugate, violate:--bring into bondage, force, keep under, subdue, and bring into subjection (Strong's Talking Greek & Hebrew Dictionary, 2017). God gave them dominion over everything that existed. However, when Adam and Eve disobeyed God and ate from the tree of good and evil, their power to subdue the earth and have dominion was gone. Adam's sin caused him to relinquish his power. The punishment for disobedience was severe. *"Unto the woman he said, I will greatly multiply thy sorrow and thy conception; in sorrow thou shalt bring forth children; and thy desire shall be to thy husband, and he shall rule over thee"* (Gen. 3:16). The husband would rule over his wife. The word rule here is the Hebrew word, mashal, which means to have dominion, governor, reign, or have power (Strong's Talking Greek & Hebrew Dictionary, 2017). Therefore, the transgression had grave consequences.

Of all the forces loose in the land, I detest a controlling force. This force is the most dangerous and damaging. Control is a force that will try to modify behavior or actions through fear, manipulation, or intimidation. When you yield to the controlling force, you empower the controller to oppress you. The same force is behind prejudice. (The Holy Ghost explained prejudice in this manner. He said, "The problem is not with color, but with dominance").

One person's desire to dominate (rule) another is a powerful motivator. Over the years, I have observed that certain personality types tend to control more than others do. For example, a parent may exhibit such extreme control over a child that the child takes on different characteristics just to appease the domineering parent. Husbands have often inflicted great pain on wives through the control of their actions. Wives are so fearful that they are unable to make simple decisions without the husband's consent or without anticipating the husband's reaction to the decision. Control is not of God.

How do you know when you are under the influence of a controlling force? Your countenance and attitude change when a person enters the room. Let me explain. You and a friend are delightfully engaged in a conversation, and you are very cheerful. Suddenly, the atmosphere changed when your husband or wife walked into the room. All laughter ceased, and a more somber demeanor came upon you. You are under the influence of that controlling force.

If your spouse tracks how long it takes to get from work to home and reprimands you for being late, that's control. A controlling person tries to usurp authority. He or she may try to remake the person into someone that God did not create. They think motivation happens best through criticism and negative actions. For the controller, punishment is the order of the day. They mold a person by withholding affection or praise. Driven by the need to control, the controller would work and work until he or she modifies behavior.

Severe instances of control can drain the life out of a person. A person can become depressed, almost catatonic. Control works whether the person is in or out of the presence of the controller. Despair and hopelessness occur. How do you break the power of the controlling force? You bind the fear. For a person controlled, fear must be the cause. There is a fear of losing the spouse, fear of disapproval, or fear of losing privileges. Even employers control employees through fear of losing their jobs. Why does anyone allow themselves to be controlled? *"... They loved the praise of men more than the praise of God" (John 12:43).* We are always trying to please someone else. We cannot measure up to the standards set by the person; yet, we aim to please.

Even in the Bible, the scribes and Pharisee tried to control the apostles. I like what the apostles said when they were threatened and told not to teach anymore in the name, Jesus. Acts 4:17-19 states, *"But that it spread no further among the people, let us straitly threaten them, that they speak henceforth to no man in this name. 18 And they called them, and commanded them not to speak at all nor teach in the name of Jesus. 19 But Peter and John answered and said unto them, Whether it be right in the sight of God to hearken unto you more than unto God, judge ye."* The apostles' reply was simple. Ye judge, men, whether we should obey you or obey God. They warned them not to preach; yet, they continued to walk in freedom. Acts 5:*17-20* states, *"Then the high priest rose up, and all they that were with him, (which is the sect of the Sadducees,) and were filled with indignation, 18 And laid their hands on the apostles, and put them in the common prison. 19 But the angel of the Lord by night opened the prison doors, and brought them forth, and said, 20 Go, stand and speak in the temple to the people all the words of this life."* They enjoyed their liberty in Christ and continued to preach. As a result, they were imprisoned. However, the angel of the Lord set them free and commanded them to continue to speak "all the words of this life."

When the apostles appeared before the council, the men said, *"Did not we straitly command you that you should not teach in this name? And behold, ye have filled Jerusalem with your doctrines, and intend to bring this man's blood upon us Then Peter and the other apostles answered and said, We ought to obey God rather than men" (Acts 5:28).* The apostles decided not to yield to the control. They held fast to their conviction and remained faithful to God.

The force, control, must be broken. It is not God's will for any human being to dominate another. All over the world, there are men and women who are under the force of control. Whoever you are, God wants you free from the bondage of control. He wants you to have life and experience joy. Jesus gave you life, and that signifies He approves of you.

Take a moment now to reflect on your situation. Change your mind regarding allowing someone to control you. Settle it in your mind that you want to be free from the bondage of control. This decision must be an act of your will. You must take authority and responsibility for your actions and your life. Say, I break the power of the controlling force over my life now in the name of Jesus. I want to LIVE! Thank you, Jesus, for setting me free. Your stronghold is severed in the spirit. I encourage you not to feel guilty. Do not be lured back into the controlling situation. Find a scripture to stand on such as John 8:36 which states, *"If the Son therefore shall make you free, ye shall be free indeed."* Remember, the power to be free is in the name of Jesus; the will to be free is in you.

Fear of Lack

Often a divorce changes your financial position. Whereas there were two incomes, now there is one. Some people stay in a marriage because they do not want to experience lack. Love is gone. It is now just a financial arrangement under the guise of marriage. Most people are not prepared for a divorce mentally, spiritually, emotionally, financially, or physically. It takes one or both parties by surprise, and they are not prepared financially to handle a breakup. Perhaps, you are receiving child support or alimony, but it is still not enough. The fear of lack left unchecked is a pathway to being poor. Remember, fear draws to you what you don't want to happen. You can change your circumstances by changing your thoughts and actions. Stop the force of fear. It gains momentum because it feeds on thoughts.

Why does poverty binds a person? Poverty is a yoke of bondage. The force of fear produces that bondage. With poverty, the yoke connects you until it brakes. It is amazing that sometimes a person can have an abundance of finances, yet the force of poverty governs decisions and actions as if the circumstances of poverty still existed.

You see the yoke still exists. How do you get free from this force? Well, the cause of poverty is fear. There is a fear of not having enough. From this fear, one tends to hoard things, become a miser, or spend foolishly from desperation. Somehow, people link poverty to self-worth.

Poverty is an image problem. Sometimes poverty is linked to grief because people lacked when they grew up. Poverty or the force of it does not just mean money or the drain of it; it could be the drain of emotions as well. People can be emotionally bankrupt. Poverty is symbolic of a void in one's life. To combat the onslaught of poverty we overcompensate. When adults who grew up in poverty become parents, either they give too much to their children to compensate for their lack, or they transfer that state of poverty into their families. Regardless of the situation, the root is fear.

The Word tells us that God has not given us the spirit of fear. So, why are you obeying the devil? Remember, you must cast out fear. God gives us power, love, and a sound mind to overcome fear. Combat the spirit of fear with the Word of God. You must arm yourself with scriptures that counteract that fear of lack.

Sometimes friends, peers, relatives and the environment paint a picture that a lifestyle of poverty is acceptable. Have you been around people who consider poverty as a source of humility? Somehow, the message is conveyed that being poor honored God. It is like the cliché, "cleanliness is next to godliness." We have been brainwashed by sayings and teachings that are not scriptural. Hosea 4:6 states: *6 "My people are destroyed for lack of knowledge."* Destroyed for lack of knowledge is a strong statement. Ignorance of the Word destroys people. I have heard people say, What you don't know can't hurt you. However, I disagree. If you don't know what the Word says, you will live a defeated life.

If you don't know your rights and privileges as a Christian, you cannot receive your inheritance. *"For ye know the grace of our Lord Jesus Christ, that, though he was rich, yet for your sakes he became poor, that ye through his poverty might be rich" (2 Cor. 8:9).* What great love Jesus bestowed upon us? He took our poverty and gave us His riches. Through his love and grace, He demonstrated what belongs to all who are in Christ. It is important to know and understand that Jesus did everything for us because of relationship. He became poor so that we might become rich.

God's will for us is to not to be poor but to prosper. First look at the promise given to Abraham. Genesis 12:*2-3* states, *"And I will make of thee a great nation, and I will bless thee, and make thy name great; and thou shalt be a blessing: 3 And I will bless them that bless thee, and curse him that curseth thee: and in thee shall all families of the earth be blessed."* All families are blessed because of the faithfulness of Abraham. *"So then they which be of faith are blessed with faithful Abraham" (Gal. 3:9). "And if ye be Christ's, then are ye Abraham's seed, and heirs according to the promise" (Gal. 3:29).* God said to Abraham, I will bless thee. The wealth, riches, and blessings were God's gift to Abraham. All he had to do was say thank you. All the promises made to Abraham extend to us. We are heirs with him according to the promise. Like Abraham, we must be faithful and walk in faith.

Replace the void in your finances with scriptures like Deuteronomy 8:18. It plainly tells us that God gives us the power to get wealth. For those who think being rich will make you lose your salvation, this scripture is for you.

Psalms 112:3 reassures us that we can be rich and righteous all at the same time. Quote and feed your spirit man on Verse 3, *"Wealth and riches shall be in his house: and his righteousness endureth for ever."* Your right standing with God is based on better promises than wealth. Righteousness is free; it is a gift from Jesus. You cannot do a thing to declare yourself righteous.

Wealth is a covenant promise. The reason we are not walking in that covenant promise is fear and disobedience. The Word said wealth and riches "shall" be in your house. Riches are an abundance of possessions and affluence; wealth is the accumulation of those riches. Both wealth and riches are available to you. Also, *Isaiah 45:3 states, "And I will give thee the treasures of darkness, and hidden riches of secret places, that thou mayest know that I, the LORD, which call thee by thy name, am the God of Israel."* Notice again that the Word confirms the will of God concerning wealth and riches. He said he would give us the treasures of darkness and hidden riches. To receive the promise, we must activate our faith to believe and trust God. Do not let fear steal your finances.

God will provide for you. Many scriptures are available for you to stand on concerning finances. Deuteronomy 28:1-14 explains the blessings of obedience and promises of the Lord. My favorite of these scriptures is verse two, which states, *"And all these blessings shall come on thee, and overtake thee, if thou shalt hearken unto the voice of the Lord thy God."* All we need to do is obey the Word to receive these blessings from God. Another scripture that I activate in my life is regarding tithing. The Word says, *"Bring ye all the tithes into the storehouse, that there may be meat in mine house, and prove me now herewith, saith the Lord of hosts, if I will not open you the windows of heaven, and pour you out a blessing, that there shall not be room enough to receive it" (Mal 3:10).* While obeying and eliminating the fear of lack, we need to activate the promise of God concerning tithing. What is the tithe? Most people think the tithe is about money so they ignore the concept, especially when they do not have any money. However, it is not about the money; it is about the relationship. God instituted the tithe as a commandment for the children of Israel to provide for the operation of the temple and the people responsible for overseeing its care. The amount given as the tithe was a tenth. God considers the gift of the tithe as holy and dedicated to Him. Leviticus 27:32 declares that the *"tenth shall be holy unto the Lord."* Since it is presented unto Him, He receives and blesses it. The tithe becomes a covenant between God and His people. Therefore, He makes the proclamation of what He will do for those who honor Him with the tithe. God said He would pour out a blessing that there would not be room enough to receive if we obeyed the commandment to tithe. Furthermore, He said he would rebuke the devour for our sakes (Mal. 3:11). Anything that tries to devour your finances, God will rebuke. Is your drain clogged or flowing freely? Now is a good time to add to your budget line the ten percent of your income that you will contribute unto the Lord. Ask God for wisdom in managing your finances.

Guard your thoughts and your heart by removing negativity. Do not speak lack out of your mouth. When you constantly say how broke you are, those words work against you to make sure you do not have enough. Release your faith to dare to believe God for what you need. Be a good steward and accountable for the funds you have today. Have a plan and work the plan. Have a budget and stick to it. Save even when you don't have enough. Give, even when you don't have enough. These two actions speak volumes in the spirit realm. It declares I trust God to supply my need according to His riches in glory by Christ Jesus (Phil. 4:19). Lastly, remember, your salary does not define you; it is just one of the tools used to bless you.

Bound by Worry

Worry is a sense of anxiousness and a fear of the unknown. When you worry, your thoughts consume you. No matter how you try, you cannot take your mind off the thing. The Word of God teaches us that we cannot change one thing by worrying about it. We cannot add or take away anything by simply spending all our time thinking about it. Matthew 6:34 states, *"Take therefore no thought for the morrow: for the morrow shall take thought for the things of itself. Sufficient unto the day is the evil thereof."* Simply, take one day at a time and one step at a time.

Do not be anxious about the things you cannot see or control. Philippians 4:6-7 states, *"Be careful for nothing; but in every thing by prayer and supplication with thanksgiving let your requests be made known unto God. And the peace of God, which passeth all understanding, shall keep your hearts and minds through Christ Jesus."* When we have complete trust in God, we can relax and wait for an answer. Our confidence must be in God.

Worry steals our peace. Can we change the situation by worrying? No! Worry causes stress, anxiety, fear, doubt, unbelief, and confusion. You may say I can't help it; I just worry. You can help it; you can obey the Word of God. When Paul told the Christians to be careful for nothing, he meant just that. It is a command. A command means that it is something that you do. How do you stop worrying? To keep from worrying you must stay focused on Jesus. *"Thou wilt keep him in perfect peace, whose mind is stayed on thee: because he trusteth in thee. Trust ye in the LORD for ever: for in the LORD JEHOVAH is everlasting strength" (Is. 26:3-4).* When your thoughts begin to wander, bring them back into captivity by concentrating on the Word. Your thoughts try to govern your actions and your body. We often let our imagination run wild. Our goal is to stay in the place of perfect peace. We can obtain perfect peace by *"Casting down imaginations, and every high thing that exalteth itself against the knowledge of God, and bringing into captivity every thought to the obedience of Christ;" (2 Cor. 10:5).* You must guard your mind and your thoughts. Everything you need to take authority over worry is within you right now. Meditate on the Word and not your problems.

> *Finally, brethren, whatsoever things are true, whatsoever things are honest, whatsoever things are just, whatsoever things are pure, whatsoever things are lovely, whatsoever things are of good report; if there be any virtue, and if there be any praise, think on these things. 9Those things, which ye have both learned, and received, and heard, and seen in me, do: and the God of peace shall be with you (Phil. 4:8-9).*

To break the habit of worrying, we must change our thinking so we do not act on those thoughts. If we bring our thinking and speaking into alignment with the Word of God, most of the problems we thought we had would cease. Turn the situation around by obeying the Word. If you follow the instructions in Philippians on what to think, you will experience the peace of God over your mind.

Bound by Bad Habits

How can one find peace in a coffee cup? Do people drink coffee for the calming effect or the energy? According to one's body chemistry, caffeine can be a stimulant or a downer. When people are in bondage to caffeine, they must have several cups or pots of coffee, or several cokes each day. When they state they would get a headache without the caffeine, then the addiction is strong. This simple drink took control of the person and became a stronghold. Several habit-forming agents can become a stronghold in the life of the individual. Cigarettes may bind some people. I have heard people say that smoking calms them or smoking relieves the stress. When they begin smoking as many as four packs of cigarettes a day, they recognize they have a problem. They try nicotine patches, hypnosis, and other treatments, all to be free of their addiction. Alcoholism is another common stronghold. Most people start out drinking as a form of socialization. They tell me, I drink socially. Most alcoholics believe they can stop drinking anytime they want. They often state I don't have a drinking problem.

A habit or deep craving left unattended becomes an addiction. We don't often think of sweets as a problem. However, anything taken to the extreme or anything that controls a person can become addictive. Gluttony is also bondage. Excessive eating even when one is not hungry indicates a lust for food or an attempt to have control. When a person is depressed, he or she tends to eat excessively to compensate for the problem. They think the only thing they do have control over is whatever they put in their mouths. Their life is in a shamble, so they eat. This excessive eating results in weight gain and then they become even more depressed. People who are obsessed with gaining weight will suffer from either bulimia or anorexia. The fear drives them to binge or to starve themselves. The point behind these examples is to inform you that any addiction is not of God. If you fall into any one of these categories, Jesus can deliver you. The key to being free from bondage is to want to be free. Like the children of Israel who were in bondage for so long, you must want and ask for God's help. Do not get discouraged; it is God's will for you to be free.

The gift of freedom is something Jesus provided through the cross. He said, *"And ye shall know the truth, and the truth shall make you free" (John 8:32)*. The enemy works hard to keep us deceived regarding our rights and benefits as a born-again believer. He does not want us to know that we do not have to be enslaved by habits, addictions, or sin. *"Verily, verily, I say unto you, Whosoever committeth sin is the servant of sin. 35And the servant abideth not in the house for ever: but the Son abideth ever. 36 If the Son therefore shall make you free, ye shall be free indeed" (John 8:34-36).*

Living and walking in truth will always make you free. The key is how to stay free. To keep from having a relapse, you must *"Stand fast therefore in the liberty wherewith Christ hath made us free, and be not entangled again with the yoke of bondage" (Gal. 5:1)*. Ask Jesus now to set you free from the spirit of bondage.

Do you want to live an abundant life? Remember, in John 10:10 Jesus said, *"The thief cometh not, but for to steal, and to kill, and to destroy: I am come that they might have life, and that they might have it more abundantly."* How do you define an abundant life? What does it look like or represent? Bondage is a thief, and Jesus is the giver of life. His purpose on earth was to show us how to live.

Now is your hour to receive inner healing from bondage. One thing I know and have experienced is the loving kindness of our Savior. His love pierces through adversity and abounds. He can reach you wherever you reside. Often, we are overtaken by guilt, shame, and grief from

64

the bondage. We experience guilt because we feel that we let someone down or we let God down. Shame is present because the bondage was such a stronghold. Pain exists because it brought humiliation or disgrace to oneself or family. Most profound is the grief and sorrow that bondage causes. Sometimes that pain is unbearable. At this point, you must not feel sorry for yourself. You must gain strength from the Savior and hold fast as your life depends upon it. Through all the circumstances, remember, God always has a plan for deliverance. He sees your need, and He hears your cry. Likewise, when God removed the reproach of bondage from Israel, they had this testimony for their children. They spoke of the victory of deliverance from Pharaoh.

20 And when thy son asketh thee in time to come, saying, What mean the testimonies, and the statutes, and the judgments, which the LORD our God hath commanded you?

21 Then thou shalt say unto thy son, We were Pharaoh's bondmen in Egypt; and the LORD brought us out of Egypt with a mighty hand:

22 And the LORD showed signs and wonders, great and sore, upon Egypt, upon Pharaoh, and upon all his household, before our eyes:

23 And he brought us out from thence, that he might bring us in, to give us the land which he sware unto our fathers (Deut. 6:20-23).

The children of Israel testified about how God brought them out of Egypt with a mighty hand. Also, God will bring you out. The key to being victorious over any yoke of bondage is having faith in a loving God who can deliver you from bondage and set you free. All you have to do is ask Him and then follow His instructions. If the boat you were in was taking on water and it was inevitable that it would sink, you would need to get out of the boat. The instructions given were simply "jump." You would have to exercise your faith not to panic and jump. In addition, you will need to trust the person giving the instructions. That is how it is with God. You must trust Him to save you from the perils of the waters, and you need to trust Him to get you through divorce or anything else you encounter. He is here to help!

Psalms 121:1-4 is one of my favorite passages. It states:
1 1 will lift up mine eyes unto the hills, from whence cometh my help.
2 My help cometh from the Lord, which made heaven and earth.
3 He will not suffer thy foot to be moved: he that keepeth thee will not slumber.
4 Behold, he that keepeth Israel shall neither slumber nor sleep."

No Regrets

In the early years of this journey, silently within myself, I had this heaviness, remorse, disappointment, and sorrow come over me. I wondered about myself. How did I stay so long on a sinking ship? Why did I stay? Gradually, with God's help, I moved on from that place of regret.

Over the years, I learned to trust God in everything. I may not do everything right but God is perfect, and I trust Him. There were good days and some not so good days. However, through it all, I learned to trust Jesus more and more. He is my friend, and I can talk to Him about everything that happens. I am so grateful for songs like "What a Friend We Have in Jesus" by Joseph M. Scriven. The lyrics state "*Oh, what peace we often forfeit Oh, what needless pain we bear. All because we do not carry, everything to God in prayer" (1855).* First, the words to the song taught me I have a friend in Jesus. Secondly, I need not suffer alone. I do not have to bear the pain by myself; nor do I have to forego peace. There is peace in the midst of the storm when the one who spoke to the storm and calmed the raging sea is with you. My relationship with Christ is even stronger.

It is no point looking back and thinking I could have, I should have, or I would have. The truth of the matter is it does not matter now. What is important is what we do going forward? What did we learn from our mistakes or setbacks? What changes occurred because of life's detour? I have learned from the scriptures and life that nothing can happen apart from God. Romans 8:28 states: *"And we know that all things work together for good to them that love God, to them who are the called according to his purpose."* In essence, divorce did not take God by surprise. He saw us going down a path, but we were never out of His view. He watches over and waits for us to seek His direction and help. When we do, God turns a devastating situation around in our lives and allows us to see that He is always with us.

God has a plan for our lives. Because of grace, that special place in God's heart for us, He will take those hurts and pains and turn them into genuine love and compassion. He can use the decisions we made and the detour we took and shape our lives and our future in Him. *"For I know the plans I have for you, says the Lord. They are plans for good and not for evil, to give you a future and a hope"* *(Jer. 29:11, TLB).* The operative word here is a future and hope. So, do not get discouraged; God is working things out for you behind the scenes. You may ask, how can good come from brokenness? For me, the solution was to give God the pieces of my broken heart and allow Him to heal me. I suggest you do the same; it works.

In my first marriage of twelve years, two beautiful girls came because of that union. They have a wonderful relationship with their father and his family. It was important for them to see that our relationship, after divorce, was cordial, not hostile. We worked together for the good of the children. Both obtained an undergraduate college education without being in debt. Both furthered their education; one obtained a doctorate in Behavioral and Community Health and the other one became a Doctor of Veterinary Medicine. They are successful in their careers, active in ministry, and Spirit-filled believers. For this, I am eternally grateful to God.

Remarry?

Now, what I have learned from God is that marriage is spiritual and not of the flesh. During my time of brokenness from the second marriage and trying to write this book, I must have been going through and feeling guilty because the Lord posed a question to me. He asked, "Was Solomon's marriages of the flesh or the spirit?" Of course, I answered of the flesh. I remembered reading in 1 Kings 11:3 that Solomon *"had seven hundred wives, princesses, and three hundred concubines: and his wives turned away his heart."* After my response, there was silence. I guess the Lord was saying I rest my case. In other words, Debra, what more could you expect when your foundation was faulty. So, why did Solomon feel the need to have so many wives, princesses, and concubines? Did he have them for love or lust? In other words, there has to be more to a marriage than flesh.

When we enter into a relationship built on physical attraction, it will be ruled and governed by the flesh. It will be subject to the ups and downs of the flesh. Hence, I compare it to an emotional roller coaster. When marriage is of the spirit and ordained by God, it has a solid foundation. I am not saying that this is the only ingredient for a perfect marriage because it is not. It will still have imperfect people, with flaws and imperfections, uniting in matrimony to become one.

Marriage has to take into consideration first the character of the individuals. For it is in the character or lack thereof that commitment, betrayal, loyalty, and adultery resides. Emotional stability, personality, upbringing, likes and dislikes, compatibility, etc. are just some of the things considered in a relationship. Do you have anything in common? What do you talk about? When considering the pros and cons of getting married, is there anything on the list that is a deal breaker? What things do you both love to do? Do you communicate well? What type of family relationship exists? Are you both financially stable?

The second marriage was missing quite a lot before it ever began. Steeped in lies, deception, cover-ups, selfishness, jealousy, hidden things, competition, and secrets, it was doomed to fail. It is hard to know a person when you are dating. You get to see the picture that they are painting and not the old one underneath the canvas. Things were fine at the beginning of the fairytale marriage. He had charisma and I was in love. He was well liked by those in the community.

Little by little, the true nature of the person emerged. He pretended that he admired the relationship I had with my daughters. However, in reality, he was jealous of that relationship and the life they lived before him. He wanted me to himself, without my children. I remember him saying I should send them to their dad. Talking to my sister, she reminded me that God entrusted the children to me and they were my responsibility. When that did not work, he began the harassment and intimidation technique, and the thread that was holding the marriage together began to unravel.

Cover Up

As the years progressed, the severity of drinking, drugs, and women increased. Because I was not street savvy like him, he thought I believed whatever he told me. Even though I did not believe him, I was ashamed and filled with shattered hope. In bad relationships, we deny the truth even when people are hinting or making remarks. Pride caused me not to confess that this was happening. The Lord calls it providing a cloak for sin. John 15:22 states, "*If I had not come and spoken unto them, they had not had sin: but now they have no cloak for their sin.*" When you know the truth, but hide it, you are providing a cloak or cover up for the sin. You don't want others to know just how bad it is in your house.

During this time, I had prayer meetings, self-help seminars, and Bible study in my home. He was suspicious of others and their motives; I believe it was because he did not want to be exposed. It got to the point that he did not want people coming to the house visiting me. To embarrass me, he would walk through the room mumbling about our gathering. You may be in a situation where your spouse wants to separate you from your family. Caution! Pay attention to red flags. Isolation is a strategy used by the devil to keep you from people that can help. The devil's ultimate goal, of course, is to destroy whether it is physical or mental.

Everyone has a story. Some stories involve physical, verbal, and mental abuse. Others end in tragedy with a child or spouse dying or harmed. Nevertheless, for the grace of God, that was not me. However, I remember him following me to the bedroom, harassing me. He had his uniform on with his service revolver. I was angry, he baited me to take the gun, and I reached for it. I believe the look in my eyes said it all. How dangerous the situation had become, and it was spiraling out of control. I asked for a divorce, and we went to the lawyer to begin the first set of paperwork. However, we did not get very far in the process. We were in the parking lot of Sonic Drive-In one day, and he was in a fit of rage. Later that day he had a heart attack. Feeling sorry for him, I forgave him, dropped the divorce, and nursed him back to health. I was naïve to think that a close encounter with death would change him. It did not. Recovery was quick, and nothing had changed.

The divorce could have ended in a long drawn out court battle for custody or property, but it did not. All we had together was a beautiful house, furniture and a couple of vehicles. Living in Florida, I filed for a divorce in Arkansas. At first, he refused to sign any paperwork so he could hold me hostage to a marriage that neither one of us wanted. I remember the Lord said to me, "Offer him half of the sale of the house." He knew it would motivate him to sign the divorce papers. I returned to Arkansas for the divorce, and it went through without a hitch. I will never forget what my lawyer said, "Sometimes you just have to buy your way out of a marriage." That is what I did. The peace of mind was worth the cost.

Through it all, I learned to trust and depend on Jesus for everything. Andre Crouch wrote a song called, "Through it all." The lyrics have always been a comfort to me.

I thank God for the mountains,
and I thank Him for the valleys,
I thank Him for the storms He brought me through.
For if I'd never had a problem,
I wouldn't know God could solve them,
I'd never know what faith in God could do.

Like the words to the song, I thank God for showing me how faith in Him would make a difference in life. You see I could never have escaped utter destruction without God's help and divine intervention. I would not be as sensitive to the needs of others had I not experienced a lot in those years. To say that I am so grateful for all God has done and will continue to do for me does not seem adequate. The best I can do is show Him how much I love and appreciate Him by helping others along the way.

With God's help, you too can dare to live again. Help is always available. Whenever you need a friend, comforter, or companion, Jesus is there for you. He is not judging you; He prays for you. Romans 8:34 states, *"Who is he that condemneth? It is Christ that died, yea rather, that is risen again, who is even at the right hand of God, who also maketh intercession for us."* I like to think of Jesus sitting at the right hand of God having a conversation about us. Think of that the next time you feel dismayed and take comfort in the fact that Jesus prays for you.

CHAPTER FIVE
LIVE LIFE

I t is now time to write a new chapter in your life. You have the opportunity to "reach" beyond where you are and stretch your faith to where you want to go. Destiny awaits your next move. The past is behind you; it is time to dare to dream again. Wherever you are in life, He can help you get your life back on track. Turn the pages in your book of life. After brokenness, trials, adversity, disappointment, shame, regret, and hardship, take the next step and learn to live again. You have so much life inside of you. Survival mode is not an option.

What does it mean to live? I mean really live. If you want to know how to live, look at Jesus. He fulfilled His purpose and did everything that God sent Him to do. Jesus' testimony was that "*I do always those things that please him" (Jn. 8:39).* In John 17:4, he told the Father, "*I have glorified thee on the earth: I have finished the work which thou gavest me to do.*" He could not leave this earth without accomplishing all that was written about Him. I encourage you today do not go to your grave without accomplishing all that you were sent here to do. You have the power within to be or do whatever you set your mind and heart to do. Therefore, there are no excuses for the body of Christ to live a defeated life. We have one enemy working against our faith. It is the same enemy of our Father, Satan. His strategy is always the same. He wants us to have doubt, fear, and absolutely no faith. The good news is this, what Jesus accomplished on the cross destroyed the works of the devil. Therefore, sin has no dominion over those who are in Christ. From the foundation of the world, God made provision to redeem man. Sin separated us from God's presence, and Jesus' death reconciled us back to Him. Colossians 1:19-20 states, *"For it pleased the Father that in him should all fulness dwell; 20 And, having made peace through the blood of his cross, by him to reconcile all things unto himself; by him, I say, whether they be things in earth, or things in heaven.*

Through His death, burial, and resurrection, He put away sin. Therefore, His death is a gift of eternal life. We must accept the gift and say thank you. Our right standing is due to the blood of Jesus. He gave us an opportunity to live life victoriously in Him. Next, Christ taught us how to live this present life of abundance through His Word. It is apparent to me that the spoken word is powerful. Jesus used the Word of God to counteract a confrontation with the devil. Let's look at the strategy used in Luke 4:1-4:

4:1 And Jesus being full of the Holy Ghost returned from Jordan, and was led by the Spirit into the wilderness, 2 Being forty days tempted of the devil. And in those days he did eat nothing: and when they were ended, he afterward hungered. 3 And the devil said unto him, If thou be the Son of God, command this stone that it be made bread.
4 And Jesus answered him, saying, It is written, That man shall not live by bread alone, but by every word of God.

The way to combat the negative is with the positive and powerful Word of God. Satan tempted Jesus through his flesh concerning hunger; he responded through the Spirit with the Word of God. When faced with adversity, you must use the same weapon Christ used. Declare to the enemy it is written. *"For the weapons of our warfare are not carnal, but they are mighty through God to the pulling down of strongholds" (2 Cor. 10:4).* Some of the weapons we can use in warfare include the Word, the blood, and the name of Jesus. Satan is not Lord; Jesus is Lord. As

our Lord and Savior, Jesus has given every believer
authority over the devil and his deeds.

Power to the Believer

Jesus gave us the authority to use His name to make the
demons subject to us. The devil only pretends to have all
power. However, the truth is he only acts on the power
that others release to him by not knowing who they are in
Christ. When a born-again believer applies faith, the name
of Jesus, and the Word of God, he or she can defeat the
enemy on every hand. Jesus admonished us to walk in the
authority that He delegated to us. When seventy disciples
were sent to evangelize, they walked in the same power
that Jesus delegated to the twelve disciples. Their
instructions were to *"Heal the sick, cleanse the lepers,
raise the dead, cast out devils: freely ye have received,
freely give"* (Mt. 10:8). *"And the seventy returned again
with joy, saying, Lord, even the devils are subject unto us
through thy name"* (Lk. 10:17). They were victorious and
excited about what they experienced. Jesus' reply to their
good report was this:

*19 Behold, I give unto you power to tread on serpents and
scorpions, and over all the power of the enemy: and
nothing shall by any means hurt you.
20 Notwithstanding in this rejoice not, that the spirits are
subject unto you; but rather rejoice, because your names
are written in heaven (Lk.10:19-20).*

The first word for power in Luke 19 is exousia. Exousia is
a Greek word that means privilege, force, capacity,
competency, freedom, or delegated influence: --authority,
jurisdiction, liberty, power, right, and strength (Strong's
Talking Greek & Hebrew Dictionary, 2017). Jesus gave
us the authority, privilege, and freedom to use His name to

subdue the enemy. He said we have power over all the power of the enemy. What does all this mean to you and me? Jesus said all and He meant it. All power belongs to us; it is time to use it.

The second word, power, was dunamis. The Greek word dunamis means miraculous power:--ability, abundance, meaning, might, mighty deed, (worker of) miracle(-s), power, strength, violence, mighty (wonderful) and work (Strong's Talking Greek & Hebrew Dictionary, 2017). Jesus gave us power over all the exploits and deeds Satan would use to deceive the body of Christ. Satan is defeated. We must always walk in that knowledge. We must recognize the fact that the greater one lives inside of us. *"Ye are of God, little children, and have overcome them: because greater is he that is in you, than he that is in the world" (1 Jn. 4:4).*

The greater one helps us to prosper in whatever we purpose to do. We can have confidence in the authority Jesus gave to us. He reassures us that nothing shall by any means hurt us. We do not have to fear the devil. We must tread on him and all his works. Victory is ours because of Jesus.

When we know and walk in authority, we understand fully who we are in Christ Jesus and who we can become. We are not a defeated foe; we are an overcomer. In 1 Peter 5:8-9, we are warned to:

8 Be sober, be vigilant; because your adversary the devil, as a roaring lion, walketh about, seeking whom he may devour:
9 Whom resist stedfast in the faith, knowing that the same afflictions are accomplished in your brethren that are in the world.

The devil is not a ferocious lion; he is only pretending to be one. He is not omnipresent. He cannot be in all places at the same time. God is the only omnipotent, omnipresent one. You have the creator of the universe on your side watching over you, protecting you, and keeping you safe from harm. The Holy Spirit is your life coach, comforter, protector, and counselor. He is present always to guide, direct, and gently lead you in the direction you should go. You have His voice on the inside of you that steer you in the right direction. Often, people will say something told me to do this or not to do that. We now know that is was not something but someone, the Holy Spirit. Jesus is seated at the right side of the Father in heaven interceding for you to be victorious.

One Day at a Time

Where do you start? Are there hopes and dreams that you put on a shelf when you were in survival mode? If there are, then start there. Get up, dust yourself off, dust off those dreams, and rekindle the fire that once burned. Do you need to pursue a career? Do not be afraid. Look within yourself and remember what you loved to do. You were once passionate about something. If necessary, take a course. If you have a hobby that you love to do, let that hobby become your business. The main point I am trying to make is "do something." Regain your self-worth and dignity; be bold and confident. Draw from God's strength that is inside you now. Change your thoughts, your attitude, and your words. A daily confession should be "*I can do all things through Christ which strengtheneth me*" *(Phil. 4:13)*. Don't talk yourself out of doing things; push yourself. Set goals. Have a plan and work the plan. I know you feel that you have no strength, but you do. The joy of the Lord is your strength.

Power in Joy

Have you forgotten how good it feels to laugh? I remember how much fun my girls and I had laughing and doing things. When my husband would come in the room, the atmosphere would shift. Everyone would become very serious. If that was you, you are free to laugh. Even in the midst of the storm, laugh. *"My brethren, count it all joy when ye fall into divers' temptations; Knowing this, that the trying of your faith worketh patience. But let patience have her perfect work, that ye may be perfect and entire, wanting nothing" (Js. 1:1-4).* "Count it all joy" encourages us not to see the trials and tribulations surrounding the situation, but see Jesus as the solution. If we look at the problem through the eyes of joy, it will not be that bad. Joy gives us the power to release the problem or situation.

Count on Jesus to help. Mark 5:25-28 tells the story of a woman who had an appointment with destiny. For twelve years, she had an issue of blood. She had seen many physicians, spent all her money, and still was not healed. In fact, she grew worse. What I like about the woman is that she persevered. She did not accept a bad report; she looked for a solution. When she heard of Jesus, she said, *"If I may touch but his clothes, I shall be whole" (Mk.5:28).* This statement was her confession of faith. It was not just words to her; it was a goal, and she took action. She prepared for an encounter with Jesus, the healer. By pushing her way through the crowd, she reached for Jesus' garment and touched it. Immediately, the issue of blood dried up. In that moment, everything changed for her; she received life without sickness or disease. Patiently waiting, without giving up, she received a fresh start. Since I know that with God nothing happens by chance, this was the set day for her miracle. She was in the right place at the right time.

Patience is one of the main components in life. She teaches us that we have to pace ourselves. *"The race is not given to the swift" (Eccl. 9:11).* It is not always the one who can run fast that wins. Endurance, perseverance, and consistency are characteristics of one that trains to win. What I have found is that we cannot make time nor patience hurry. They work together to perfect us. The key to waiting patiently to receive anything is to do it with joy.

Destiny Awaits

Each one of us has a path to follow and purpose in life. It is part of our destiny. When God created us, He had greatness in mind. *"For I know the plans I have for you, says the Lord. They are plans for good and not for evil, to give you a future and a hope" (Jer. 29:11 TLB).* I like to think that the plan that God has is a blueprint for living life. He gives us opportunity and allows us to make our own decisions. We have freedom to choose our path. Based on the information we have at hand and our desires, we choose. Sometimes the path chosen is not good for us. Nevertheless, we choose.

God wants the best for us. Just like any parent, we want the best for our children. We give our children room to grow, explore, and discover who they are and what they want to be when they grow up. There are no limits placed on our children nor does Father God place limits on us. In their quest to discover who they are, sometimes they take a detour and veer from the path. The detour may require them to take a different exit ramp or loop. After passing through emotional speed traps, going around discouraging curves, and traveling on single lanes, they make it. The journey was not intended to kill them or make them bitter, but it will make them wiser.

As mentioned previously, Joseph was governor in Egypt and helped his family during the time of famine. I want to share with you the perils and path Joseph was on to get to that position. Genesis Chapters 37 to 50 records the story. At the age of 17, Joseph had a dream, and it revealed future events that would take place, which he shared, with his brothers and father. The brothers hated him more because of the dream. From that time forward, they plotted to kill the dreamer to prevent the dream from coming to pass. They threw him into a pit but later decided to sell him to the Ishmaelites that were going to Egypt. Upon arrival, Joseph was sold to Potiphar, an officer of Pharaoh and captain of the guard.

The Lord was with Joseph, and he prospered in Egypt. He became an overseer of all that Potiphar owned. However, Potiphar's wife tried to seduce him. Joseph refused her advances, not wanting to sin against God. She accused him falsely, and he was cast into prison. Even in prison, the Lord gave Joseph mercy and favor. He became a director of the ward. Not only was Joseph a dreamer, God gave him the ability to interpret dreams. When Pharaoh had a dream, Joseph interpreted the dream regarding the upcoming famine. By the age of 30, Joseph was released from prison, appointed overseer of Pharaoh's house, and became second in command over all of Egypt. God divinely orchestrated Joseph's life and positioned him in Egypt to save not just his family but also a nation. The path was not easy, but he stayed the course. Joseph was 110 when he died after fulfilling his destiny.

Look back over your life. Can you trace the crooks and turns that you took that worked out for you? They may not have felt good when you encountered them. Because of those turns, you developed character, obtained wisdom, learned new skills, advanced to leadership, and achieved success. Perhaps, you are in the midst of your journey, and you have not arrived at your final destination. To keep from fainting and giving up before obtaining the victory, see Jesus. He is the author and finisher of our faith. He showed, by example, how to endure the cross, despise the shame, and receive our place. Joy is the key to help us look beyond what we go through and see the results. Consider the work of the cross and all that Christ endured to redeem and reconcile us to the Father. Jesus suffered, but He thought the sacrifice was worth the pain. We were worth it.

Breathe

Life is about choices. Each choice we make has consequences. Deuteronomy 30:19 states, *"I call heaven and earth to record this day against you, that I have set before you life and death, blessing and cursing: therefore choose life, that both thou and thy seed may live:"* The decisions you make not only affect you but your children also. Rome wasn't built in a day, nor will your life be rebuilt in a day. You have shared your life with someone for several years. It is important that you are patient with yourself and your family. I know you want to show others that you are fine. However, let the healing process take place. Breathe. Exhale all the poison of the past. It is like clearing the clutter from a house or garage during spring cleaning. Once cleared, inhale the peace of God.

Peace is such a wonderful gift. Jesus said, *"Peace I leave with you, my peace I give unto you: not as the world giveth, give I unto you. Let not your heart be troubled, neither let it be afraid" (Jn. 14:27).* Jesus gave us His

81

peace to keep and sustain us during the rough times. We must take every precaution to keep our hearts from being troubled or afraid. Moving forward let's follow King Solomon's instructions, *"Above all else, guard your affections. For they influence everything else in your life"* *(Prov. 4:23, TLB)*.

What did I do to learn to live again? I embraced life. I do those things that I love to do. I teach and give hope to hurting people. I try to relate to the pain and suffering because my mission in life is to "help others prosper and excel." With that in mind, I teach others to do more than just cope but to live. Using the scripture as a basis for life, I conduct seminars that empower others to live victoriously. More importantly, I pray for them. I know the power of prayer, and it makes a difference in life when we trust and believe.

I pray that you are ready to live again. You are no longer full of anger, sorrow, grief, regret, disappointment, unforgiveness, and the list goes on. When you empty out and let go, you make room for all the wonderful blessings God gives.

Now breathe. Your future is brighter because your new life begins now. Enjoy the journey! Without restraints, you can Reach-Destiny Awaits.

References

1. Hoffman, Elisha. A. (1893). I Must Tell Jesus.
2. Rose Kennedy. (n.d.). BrainyQuote.com. Retrieved June 27, 2017, from BrainyQuote.com https://www.brainyquote.com/quotes/quotes/r/rose kenned597699.html
3. Treason. (n.d.). Dictionary.com Unabridged. Retrieved June 30, 2017 from Dictionary.com http://www.dictionary.com/browse/treason
4. Grief. (2017). In Strong Talking Greek & Hebrew Dictionary. Retrieved from WordSearch.
5. Fiery trial. (2017). In Strong Talking Greek & Hebrew Dictionary. Retrieved from WordSearch.
6. Tribulation. (2017). In Strong Talking Greek & Hebrew Dictionary. Retrieved from WordSearch.
7. Egypt. (2017). In James Strong, Strong Talking Greek & Hebrew Dictionary. Retrieved from WordSearch.
8. Control. (n.d.). Dictionary.com Unabridged. Retrieved June 27, 2017 from Dictionary.com http://www.dictionary.com/browse/control
9. Subdue. (2017. In Strong Talking Greek & Hebrew Dictionary. Retrieved from WordSearch.
10. Rule. (2017. In Strong Talking Greek & Hebrew Dictionary. Retrieved from WordSearch.
11. Scriven, Joseph M. (1855). What A Friend We Have in Jesus.
12. Crouch, A. (1993) Through It All, Album: Classic, Vol. 1.
13. Power. (2017. In Strong Talking Greek & Hebrew Dictionary. Retrieved from WordSearch.

PRAYER FOR SALVATION

Heavenly Father I come to you just as I am. I make no pretense about where I have been or what I have done because you know everything. I do not want to live like this anymore. With my whole heart, I turn from my sins and turn to you today. Please forgive me for everything I have done that was against you and your Word. I did things that offended you. By doing this, I rejected your love and mercy for me. For that, I am truly sorry.

Father, you made provision for me to have eternal life and that life is in your Son. I believe Jesus died on the cross and shed His blood for me so that I may not die and go to hell. I believe God that you raised Christ from the dead and He is seated at your side.

This very moment I ask Jesus Christ to come into my heart to be my Lord and Savior. I receive this gift of life. According to the Word, right now, I am born again. I am a new creature in Christ; I am saved. Thank you.

Congratulations! Your new life in Christ and a closer walk with God begins now. Develop a very personal and intimate relationship with Him through prayer and reading the Bible each day. Find a good Bible-based church that preaches, teaches, and obeys the Word. Get involved and become a strong follower of Christ. Most importantly, learn and receive all the benefits and blessings that you have in Christ and share that with others.

Let's stay connected. You may contact me: Apostle Debra Allen, PO Box 822295, Pembroke Pines, FL 33082 or go online and complete the New Believer Card at www.nhwofl.org, and select online church. I would love to hear from you.

FROM THE AUTHOR

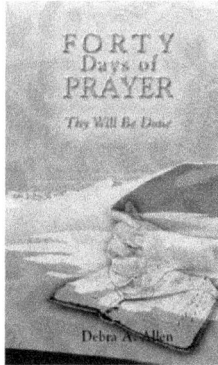

Forty Days of Prayer is a book filled with inspirational messages to help you grow in your prayer life and your relationship with God. It is a journey designed to lead you through discovery and renewed confidence in the fact that God answers prayer. Through the teachings of faith, trust, obedience, and seeking God, Apostle Debra Allen challenges you to apply the principles learned to your life of prayer.

The book is available on the website of:

www.debraallen.org or www.resources-solutions.com

For conferences, seminars, and training contact Apostle Allen at 954-907-5462 or email: drdallen@nhwo.org.

www.ingramcontent.com/pod-product-compliance
Lightning Source LLC
Chambersburg PA
CBHW072153020426
42334CB00018B/1983